Integrative Intelligence Coaching Manual

Elevating Human Potential

Through the Art & Science of

Masterful Coaching

Laurel Alison Elders

Published by
Hybrid Global Publishing
301 E 57th Street
4th Floor
New York, NY 10022

Manufactured in the United States of America.

Elders, Laurel
Integrative Intelligence Coaching Manual: Elevating Human Potential Through the Art & Science of Masterful Coaching
ISBN: 978-1-951943-71-4
eBook: 978-1-951943-72-1

Cover design by: Natasha Clawson
Copyediting by: XCU Agency
Interior design by: Suba Murugan
Author photo by: Michelle Owens

www.IntegrativeCoachTraining.com

www.IntegrativeIntelligence.global

This work is dedicated to Sandy Hogan.
May 14, 1950 - Sept. 21, 2019

Dear Beloved Sandy:
"We are the torch-holders of your profound wisdom, inspirational teachings,
and brilliant coaching legacy.
We continue to deliver the highest caliber coaching in your honor.
We were blessed to have had you with us from the start, a brick in the
foundation of our heart."

I'd like to wholeheartedly thank my mentor and our Director of Training, Nancy Smyth for years of holding space, sharing your love and being a key support in my life and work.

Thank you to our phenomenal contributors who invited this work to reach new potentials! I am deeply grateful to Nancy Smyth, Howie Adams, Michelle Weston, Megan Daley, Judi Olivas, Jessica Gammell, and Ruth Abraham.

TABLE OF CONTENTS

Accountability - Affirmation - Accomplishment - Awakenings
Believing in Self - Breakthroughs - Branching Out
Clarity - Courage - Centering - Celebrating Challenge
Dedication to Outcomes - Developing new Strategies
Embarking Anew - Empowerment - Enjoyment of Life - Expansion
Forward Movement
Feeling: Happy, Fulfilled and Engaged Guidance
Goals - Gifts to World - Gauging Success - Grounding
How To - Holding Long-term Success - Honoring What Is – Hiring a Partner
Idea generating - Inspiration - Insights - Integrity - Ingredients for Success
Journeying into New Potentials - Jumping to new Ideas
Keeping Promises to Self – Kindling new Projects – Knowledge Base Expansion
Leaving a Legacy - Life Balance - Life Purpose - Life Fulfillment
Manifestation - Motivation - Masterminding - Magnifying
New Possibilities Neutralizing Negatives - Nurturing Self Realizations
Outside the Box Thinking - Organizing Thoughts & Actions
Paradigm Shifting - Possibility Exploration - Professional Development
Quality of Life - Questions - Quenching the Thirst for Life!
Reflection - Resources - Responding vs. Reacting
Social Fluency - Structure - Strategic Planning - Success Tracking
Trying New Approaches Out - Timing - Taming the Inner-Critic
Unstuckness - Understanding - Unlocking Wisdoms - Unleashing Potentials
Value Inventorying - Visualizing - Vocalizing
Welcoming New Possibilities - Widening Self-perspective - Walking
with Wisdom
Xcellence - Xamining Needs - Xchanging Old Approaches for New Ones
Yeilding to What Is - Yearning for More
Zest and Zeal for Life - Zeroing in on Pathways to Potentials

CHAPTER ONE

❧ The Manual & Lessons ❧

There are a variety of rock climbers, and then there are adventure climbers. Adventure climbers are rock climbers who take rock climbing to the next level. Rock climbers seek established climbing routes to climb. Adventure climbers look at a rock face or mountain, discover a new aspiration to climb, and say, "Let's climb that."

Years ago, my friends, my daughter, and I set out for an adventure climb. We were visiting White Sands, New Mexico. While driving one afternoon, we saw the most beautiful rock face off in the distance and said, "Let's climb that!"

The next day we prepared and set out to reach this beautiful rock face in the distance.

We had two pre-teens in tow, kids, a baby in a backpack, and four adults. The road we were on landed us about two to three miles out from the rocks we spotted just yesterday. We parked, viewed the landscape, loaded the gear, and began the trek.

The terrain started out spacious. There were a few desert-type plants that speckled the landscape. We had high hopes and no reason to feel overly cautious.

About three-fourths of the way there, the terrain suddenly changed.

The desert landscape turned into harsh prickly bushes that consisted of large prickly thistle plants. They hurt to push through. We had to pick up the kids and hoist them over the painful brush. We had to take off our backpacks and push through the brush to avoid getting scraped. The kids were rightfully whining and upset.

We looked back and wondered if it was worth it to turn around. We seemed so close.

One of our crew ran up a hill just ahead of us to see how much more of this wretched terrain we had to put up with.

He then burst out laughing! I thought, *What on God's green planet could be so darn funny at this point!* He motioned for us to come and see.

I made my way up the hill.

What was right next to the big beautiful rock face? A parking lot.

Moral of the story? Get the lay of the land before proceeding. When you do things the hard way, you may be too tired to enjoy the climb. The path of least resistance gets you much, much farther.

This manual was written with the lay land in mind. We cover everything from the big-picture potentials embedded in Integrative Intelligence to the inner nuances of masterful coaching. We also cover the critical components to succeeding as a coach.

AUTHOR'S MESSAGE

I am so thrilled that you are here!

If you are reading this, I know that you are a person who cares about evolving your excellence in your own life and helping others to do the same. I know that you care about being a part of the solution and empowering the lives of the people who you touch.

Thank you for being here.

My mentor, Sandy Hogan, taught me that people come to coaching when something inside of them is ready to awaken. I have found this to be true for both coaches obtaining training and clients who seek a coach.

I'll ask you, "What within you is ready to awaken?"

It may be something conscious and ready to pop! Or, there may be something welling up inside that seems intangible.

This is one big, crazy and amazing world that we have all been born into. I'm happy to walk with you on this journey of your coaching path.

The Days of Integrative Thinking Have Arrived

Before we dive into the coaching lessons, I'm going to be brutally honest with you. I invite you to bear with me. There is a very positive message at the end, and we explore a better way together.

I'm bringing this up because there is a collective "elephant" in the room.

We are all collectively living in a world of massive pollution issues, public shootings, sex trafficking, and political division, to name a few. These were all new norms humanity faced. Deep down, I knew there was a better way.

When I was a teenager in the 80s, I looked around and literally thought to myself, "WTF?! What kind of absolute crazy nonsense have I been born into? There has to be a better way."

In 1997, the devastation of 5 astronomically growing "garbage patches" was discovered. "Garbage Patches" are gaping miles of human waste "landfills" accumulating in our oceans.

Are we proud of this? No. Yet, we are collectively living in this world together. Have you ever wondered how humanity has the power and intelligence to create anything we want, yet we are settling with creating pollution and massive economic bottlenecks?

As these stories piled up, my heart sank heavier and heavier and heavier...

I thought, "This is it! Humanity is done for. We have reached our peak, and now we are aptly headed downhill as quickly as we can. I throw in the towel."

A logical conclusion, right? Wrong. I found a bigger picture.

I am a rock climber. In adventure climbing, there is something called a false summit. A "False Summit" happens when it looks as if the peak of a climb is right in front of you. You climb to the top. Then, upon arrival, you realize the true summit is still in the distance. You couldn't see it from the ground. I realized, We, all of humanity, are at a false summit together. We are not at the top of our potential.

Why haven't we reached our human potential yet? Our technological advancements are growing faster than our emotional intelligence. We can fly to the moon, land on Mars, and I can text someone in Japan from Tucson, AZ. We have self-driven vacuum cleaners and cars that park themselves.

We haven't reached our human potential yet for three reasons:

- **Linear thinking produces linear results.** Linear thinking creates a one-sided focus that leaves out important factors. This funnel vision approach is outdated and highly inefficient if we are to head into a positive future. I speak more on this in Chapter Seven.

- **True success is success in all areas.** When we view success integratively, we see true success is success in all areas, not just one. We have settled for success in single areas in the past. This has limited the positive impact we could leave.

- **True success will come when we see integratively.** To cultivate an inspiring future, we must approach the collective, global and individual issues we face in integratively intelligent ways. Linear thinking got us where we are, and now is the perfect time in our collective evolution to pivot!

Coaches are helping shape a more positive future and inviting more significant shifts to take root. If we are to create a really profound future, it is time to stop settling, and time to start integrating!

A CASE FOR COACHING

First thing's first: coaching is profound!

I showed up ready to learn how to counsel people in my first coaching training class. I was so excited! I had always had a passion for helping people, so I naturally felt counseling was an excellent fit for my next steps.

Yep, you read that correctly. I assumed coaching was a light form of counseling. Not full- blown therapy per se but a way to advise people on life improvement. The idea of acquiring expertise in helping lit me up. At the time, I had been running support groups for single parents and teens, and I figured signing up for coach training was also a great way to get a stamp of approval for something I thought I was already doing.

Wow. Was I completely mistaken and blown away!

Little did I know that coaches are experts at empowering people. However, they take an entirely different path than the other helping professions.

After my first class, I was stumped. There was a modality where my entire role is to help people locate their inner power by helping them develop their inner wisdom? Why didn't I know about this sooner? I was hooked. This concept woke something up inside of me. I was so inspired that I even changed my degree focus from psychology to human development, concentrated in coaching.

After training, I attended a local coaching networking event and learned that my experience was typical and referred to as "catching the coaching bug." Coaching was contagious. What a positive way of thinking! Coaching was spreading through empowered individuals, companies, leaders, partners, and teams. People were falling head over heels in love with coaching!

And why not? Who likes to be told what to do?

Having someone hold a potentiated space while we vulnerably sift through fears, beliefs, and conditioned responses can leave one feeling tender. However, as the coach equally mirrors back our fullest potentials, truths, gifts, and values, we can also feel like we've come home to ourselves.

People were also falling in love with coaching because it is a seed of empowerment and has been proven to carry a very high impact, deep roots, and ample fruits.

Coaching is contagious because it is expanding, engaging, and highly effective.

EXPANDING:

The coaching industry is booming.

"The estimated global total revenue from coaching in 2015 was $2.4 billion, representing a 19% increase over the 2011 estimate." – International Coach Federation (IFC)

ENGAGING:

Coaching is brilliant because its methodology allows you to meet someone exactly where they are at and help them up-level to a higher vantage point.

Human beings are multidimensional, sentient, and capable of great things, like abstract thought. Coaching engages all of these aspects of self.

Coaching is a powerful and unique process where the client is the pilot and the professional coach is the co-pilot.

Coaching develops the whole person, engages all domains of potential, and shapes a more positive future.

EFFECTIVE:

I once saw a T-shirt that said, "Fishing is like dessert. Even when it is bad, it is still pretty good." This is coaching. Every session, a person will walk away with a minimum of one new action, perspective, belief, homework assignment, or approach.

There is no "one" in coaching. Coaching is the symbiotic wisdom of both the coach and client that leverages the client to a new potential.

*"You think because you understand "one" you must also
understand "two," because one and one make two.
But you must also understand "and."*
~ Rumi

Below are some statistics I've come across over the years that outline coaching efficacy.

In 2001, *Fortune* magazine featured "Executive Coaching – With Returns a CFO Could Love" in which it stated, "When asked for a conservative estimate of the monetary payoff from the coaching they got, these managers described an average return of more than $100,000 – or about six times what the coaching had cost their companies."

Employees at Nortel Networks estimated that coaching earned the company "a 529 percent return on investment and significant intangible benefits to the business, including the financial benefits from employee retention. Coaching boosted the overall ROI to 788%."

- Merrill C. Anderson, professor of clinical educator, Drake University, as reported in Psychology Today, January 2003.

Thirty-one managers underwent a conventional managerial training program, followed by eight weeks of one-on- one executive coaching, "which included goal setting, collaborative problem solving, practice, feedback, supervisory involvement, evaluation of end-results, and a public presentation." The training increased productivity by 22.4%. *Training and coaching increased productivity by 88%, a significantly greater gain compared to training alone.*

- Public Personnel Management; Washington; Winter 1997; Gerald Olivero; K. Denise Bane; Richard E. Kopelman

What leaders have to say about their coaching experiences:

"I absolutely believe that people, unless coached, never reach their maximum capabilities."
*-- Bob Nardelli, CEO of **Home Depot***

"I never cease to be amazed at the power of the coaching process to draw out the skills or talent that was previously hidden within an individual, and which invariably finds a way to solve a problem previously thought unsolvable."

*-- John Russell, Managing Director, **Harley-Davidson Europe Ltd.***

"What's really driving the boom in coaching is this: as we move from 30 miles an hour to 70 to 120 to 180 as we go from driving straight down the road to making right turns and left turns to abandoning cars and getting motorcycles the whole game changes, and a lot of people are trying to keep up, learn how not to fall."

-- John Kotter, Professor of Leadership, **Harvard Business School**

IN ESSENCE:

Coaching is a high-reward, heart-filling, and impact-driven approach.

As you learn how to coach, it is normal for it to feel awkward, counterintuitive, and highly unnatural in the beginning. It is the same with learning to ride a bike. Learning takes root, and coaching will feel fluid, natural, and even fun before you know it.

Coaching is results-based, action-packed, and forward-thinking. Coaching sets people up to grow and expand in new ways. Coaches are trained in core competencies. Integrative coaches are further trained in success principles, self-development skills, outcome models, and systematic approaches that yield measurable results.

A DISCLAIMER

Coaching is an art and a science. What coaching is theoretically and how to coach with mastery are two different aspects of reaching our coaching potential.

If you are new to coaching, this manual is a deep dive into the "what." You learn what coaching is, what coaching is not, what masterful coaching entails, and the psychology of self-actualization. We then explore in-depth the complexity and beautiful mystery of human life through the lens of Integrative Intelligence.

This manual is not a replacement for live training and coaching mentorship. Training and mentorship is the most effective and powerful way to learn "how" to be a masterful coach. Learning "how" to masterfully coach is beyond book learning and comes to life with skilled training, mentoring, and guided practice.

This manual will bring a coach's training and practice into new levels of understanding and is available as a deeper dive to supplement training, mentoring, and practice. The concepts explored within this manual apply equally to the new coach and complement the expanding mastery of the seasoned coach.

THE MISSION OF THE INSTITUTE

In 2009 I invited a group of successful professional coaches to convene. I was asked to help launch the new coaching program for Prescott College. I posed the question: "What didn't you receive in your coach training program that you felt would have helped you become a masterful coach sooner?" The group answered this question, first for ourselves and then branched out to interview how other coaches felt.

We identified ten common themes:

1. My school was great at marketing to me with dazzling possibilities, and then once I was in the door, I was on my own.
2. I only learned coaching basics and was left disappointed at the lack of depth.
3. Class sizes were so large that I felt lost in the shuffle.
4. Good program, but no alumni community or continuing education.
5. I felt thrown into the deep end. It was too open-ended and had little clarity of concept.
6. We had to coach in front of the entire class before knowing what coaching was, which felt humiliating.
7. Lack of instructor availability. Fishbowl learning didn't allow for personal attention or development.
8. They accepted anyone who would pay tuition, which caused a lot of disruption in the learning process when a student wasn't ready to be a coach.
9. I signed up for the school at the top of the Google search, assumed they were the best and learned they were not delivering high-quality content.
10. There was no business development help or post-graduate support.

Over the next two years, we crafted and formulated a fully in-depth and comprehensive training. We now deliver one of the most comprehensive programs in the nation.

We established:

1. Processes to support each student from admission to post-graduation support.
2. Learning in phases. Establishing a solid foundation to build new skills upon.
3. Capped class sizes that emphasize quality of training over quantity of class size.
4. Thriving alumni network of like-hearted professionals.
5. Depth of content, resources provided, and success support.
6. Small group practice sessions with a seasoned mentor. Non-judgmental atmosphere.
7. Office hours for outside of training support.
8. Application process to ensure students are ready and resourced to do the work.
9. Interview process to get to know each student and teach to their goals.
10. Upfront business support, contracting materials, and marketing tools.

We graduated our first group of coaches in 2012 and were excited to receive stellar feedback on our unique educational and high-touch approach.

Soon after, we became accredited by the International Coaching Federation (ICF). And in 2020, we served our 100th student.

We also recognize the need for integrity in the coaching profession. We draw clear and distinct lines between the modalities of coaching, counseling, and consulting. We respect the value each brings to the table of human empowerment. We support honoring the person seeking professional support by referring to the appropriate professional if coaching is not a fit. To that end, we adhere to the ICF's Coaching Code of Ethics and Accreditation Code of Conduct.

We are the Institute for Integrative Intelligence. We are on a mission to elevate human potential through the art and science of masterful coaching.

THE ROLE OF INTEGRATION

The concept of intelligence has been explored, studied, researched, and philosophized over for centuries. Oxford dictionary defines intelligence as "the ability to acquire and apply knowledge and skills."

We have many contributors to our current understanding of intelligence, including Howard Gardner's research on multiple intelligences found in the brain or cognitive intellect. Daniel Goleman's research on emotional intelligence and the Enneagram Institute's contributions to how we engage our intelligence center on understanding our ability to reach our potential as human beings.

Integrative Intelligence makes a contribution by honoring all key domains of intelligence, seeing the interconnected nature of each domain, and inviting expanded capacity in each. The integrative approach has the power to elevate all potentials individually and globally.

Before we dive into the heart of Integrative Intelligence, we will explore the key distinctions and language used.

Integrative Intelligence:

Integrative Intelligence is the awareness of, engagement of, and expansion of all of the domains of our human potential. Integrative Intelligence also elevates awareness of how we reach human potential through the wisdom of combining the domains.

For example, suppose I am tired of seeing politicians who lack integrity. I decide to be a politician with integrity. In that case, I can engage my motivational and relational domains and understand how the somatic, cognitive, and energetic domains support my aim. As we become integratively intelligent beings, we see how all domains support best practices, better outcomes and give us access to new possibilities.

It is worth noting other forms of intelligence we are not yet aware of may be discovered as we reach new integrational peaks.

The Eight Domains of Human Potential & Intelligences:

The domains of human potential are the foundation for elevating human capacity. A developed intelligence means we have expanded our capacity in that domain. In other words, when I do practices to expand my relational abilities, my capacity grows, and my potential in that domain is optimized.

The eight domains are: somatic, cognitive, emotional, energetic, relational, motivational, spiritual, and integrational.

There are also multiple intelligences carried within the capacity of the brain.

Howard Gardner's work is noted for his contribution to our understanding that human intelligence expands way beyond book smarts. He located eight primary intelligences held within the brain.

These are:
1. Linguistical: self-expression
2. Logical: quantifying concepts/formulas
3. Spatial: visualizing surroundings
4. Kinesthetic: coordinating mind/body
5. Musical: discerning pitch, tone, sound
6. Interpersonal: understanding others
7. Intrapersonal: self-understanding
8. Naturalist: reading/understanding nature

His work is worth noting as we approach human potential in the cognitive domain and how that intelligence plays out may also include the somatic domain.

For example, if someone has the cognitive gift for music, and then playing the music is orchestrated somatically.

Centers of Intelligence:

The centers of intelligence are a contribution of the work and research conducted by the Enneagram Institute. The centers represent the primary ways we operate and understand the world around us.

These are also referred to in this manual as our Centers of Wisdom. Each center is a way for the client to receive self-understanding: mind, body, and human spirit.

The theory the Enneagram offers us to consider is that we all default to living through one primary center of intelligence, or our central way of knowing.

Renee Siegel, founder of www.URPurePotential.com explains each center this way:

"We learn about ourselves and the world around us through observing, noticing, listening, understanding, and taking action. Not only do we receive this information through thinking (that is, from our heads) but also through our feelings (our heart) and by doing (through our body). In Enneagram language, we refer to those—the body, heart, and head—as the centers of intelligence. Each center provides us with valuable information.

"Your body center offers you sensate information through the five senses: sight, sound, smell, touch, and taste. Your heart center offers you emotional intelligence including being relational, engaged, and connected to one another. Your head center allows you to make meaning of the information coming from all the centers, including language, memory, imagination, planning, and more. You mentally map and strategize through the use of this center."

You have all three centers, but if you are like most people, you default to or rely heavily on just one or two of these centers. It may be that one or two of your centers are more developed and are therefore more easily accessible than the others.

"However, when you have access to all three centers and you are operating in an integrated way, your life runs more smoothly and is balanced."

The wisdom here is to invite integration and alignment of all three centers. We will journey into each of these elements and take deeper dives into the dimensions of human potential. We will also be studying the levels of integration and the variety of paths we can take.

A SPIRITUAL JOURNEY

The concept of spirituality is broad indeed.

For some, being spiritual represents religion. For others, it is a way of living more awake and aware, like my friend who refuses to step on ants. Even during the years of my youth that I was an atheist, I had adopted a spirituality by studying the ancient Eastern philosophies of Taoism and Buddhism. Later, my atheist view of my life brought me to study quantum physics. I wanted to know the broadest sense of truth and possibility available.

While I grew up searching for truth in Eastern philosophy, I was equally scared that there could be something greater than me. I found immense safety in being a surface scientist. If I couldn't touch it or measure it, it didn't exist to me and was "woo-woo." While it was convenient and felt like a huge relief at that moment, I came to find out in my twenties, that it also limited my capacity to expand my potential.

My search had one key element. I wanted the truth. What was the truth of how we got here and was there any purpose or meaning beyond the physical domain of life? How come the missing link still existed if science had all the answers?

In the most general sense, spirituality is having a connection to something bigger than the self. To me, spirituality is being open to parts of life where there is much more "than meets the eye." In a more specific sense, spirituality can be a religious or personal practice we do that connects us to the bigger picture of our lives and to others.

Our clients will all come to us with different spiritual relationships, philosophies, experiences, and practices. To be of service, we want to meet them wherever they are and help them expand from there.

Everyone gets to define the spiritual journey, if any, they embark on.

Within this manual, you will find a variety of spiritual quotes, success principles, and perspectives that support reaching human potential. The focus is not on the specific tradition, book, or philosophy. The focus is on the success principle the teaching represents.

Some of these reflections have a deep spiritual aspect, others are captured in the words of great thought leaders. Despite the origin of the words reflecting the principle, the principle exists regardless and does not require our belief for it to exist.

There have been many ancient spiritual teachings that have captured and handed down profound wisdom in human potential, long before psychology and quantum science began discovering these teachings were accurate. This text focuses on these principles and how they illuminate our path to potential.

Everyone's path to potential is unique. To that end, I want to take a moment and acknowledge that some of us have experienced trauma in the religion we grew up with. If you have experienced this, first, I am deeply sorry you went through this.

I want to confirm that in this text we will not be studying religion or any one tradition of thought. What we will be doing is exploring each human domain of potential so that we are fully aware of how we develop a healthy and thriving relationship with each domain. This includes the capacity for spiritual development, in the non-religious sense.

In this text, I view spirituality as a personal connection to that which is greater than the self. I view integrative intelligence as an indispensable component of being a masterful coach and enjoying an enriched spiritual life.

If you already connect with any spiritual aspect of life, I trust you will enjoy the correlations we explore. If you do not resonate with spirituality, I trust the exploration will lend to understanding your spiritually focused clients with greater depth and appreciation.

Just like gravity is a law of physics, there are principles that, when we align with them, expedite our successes. Or when we ignore them, success is experienced as ten times harder. In this text, we will be bridging ancient wisdom with modern-day dilemmas and the science that backs it all up.

Life is sacred. Your life is sacred. You are sacred. Sometimes we forget we are sacred and instead live scared. I invite you to consider how the sacred aspects of life are the way out of scared and into prepared.

Enjoy the journey!

CHAPTER TWO

✿ A Mission Driven Profession ✿

Coaching has taught me the value of humility, patience, purpose, and self-empowerment. The profession attracts mission-driven professionals who are ready to give back to others and be a part of the solution.

In this chapter, we will start by looking at the role coaching plays in elevating human potential. We will do a brief overview of the history of the coaching profession. We will also review the professional challenges coaches face, current trends, and the standards that strengthen this high-impact profession.

First, we will start with the journey of human potential.

THE JOURNEY TO POTENTIAL

Human potential is a journey…

On the first stretch of this journey, we can be shown the way. We may find guidance in books, spiritual mentoring, or counseling. There are times we may need to look to others for the answers that will guide us to a new understanding.

Yet, there is a time in our life when the answers provided to us may become the very box of our limitations. There comes a time when we must choose to maintain the way we have been shown or to pave the remainder of our life through our own wisdom. This is the second journey.

To truly reach our human potential, one must take the second journey. On the second journey, we move beyond the walls of external provision and begin to journey amongst the answers embedded within.

Each person carries a heart of knowing. This heart of knowing is what guides and informs the expansion of our growing.

In coaching, we act as a lantern illuminating the path of the second journey. We help clients access their true essence, to the seeds of potential embedded within aching to be born. Coaches are the Sherpas journeying with our clients to their unique personal apex.

What is their truth? What is their wisdom? What jewels are buried within their heart? What gifts are aching to be born?

In masterful coaching, we must sit in the unknowing to be of service to the client's growing.

Coaching plays an important role in reaching one's potential. To better understand coaching, let's look at the history of how coaching came to be what it is today.

A BRIEF HISTORY OF COACHING

Coaching has an origin back in the days of Socrates. The Greek philosopher asked questions that got people to think in new, out-of-the-box ways, inviting profound answers unlocked by asking powerful questions.

Fast forward to today.

In 1995, Thomas Leonard, a pioneer for formulating, formalizing, and professionalizing coaching practices, established the International Coaching Federation (ICF).

Why was coaching established as a profession? The other modalities were already taken.

Coaching was born from the realization that a budding new approach was on the scene and creating profound results. But, it was not counseling, and it was not consulting or advising. So, what was it?

If you look at the olden days, we can see where the root of the word originates. Think of a horse and buggy versus a train. A train has an established set point. A train is locked in on a pattern of travel to get you from A to B. Let's say from Tucson, Arizona, to San Diego, California. An established destination is akin to consulting and counseling. In these modalities, the route to a goal is pre-determined by the professional offering such services.

Coaching is unique. In coaching, the destination and route are established solely by the client.

Let's go back to the horse and buggy. A person hires a coach to get to where they want to go. Let's say they want to get to the fairgrounds. They could request to be dropped off at Woolworths along the way. The client establishes the destination, and the coach holds a safe and professional service that takes them to their intended destination.

The formulation of professional coaching is newer on the scene. Theoretical-based psychotherapy dates back to 801 AD. According to good' ol Google, professional management consulting was documented for the first time in the 1880s.

Today, the ICF is the global standard-setter, overseeing the accreditation of training programs and offering three levels of coaching credentials. Many companies who hire coaches require the coach to be ICF credentialed.

A NEW ELDER

Growing up, I often scratched my head and thought, "*This is it? This is what society and governments are choosing to create? We are so intelligent, so why not create better outcomes?*" I also noticed that there was a lack of wisdom surrounding me. I was not raised with a religion. My family attended an Episcopalian Church but only on Easter and Christmas Eve. As we got older, that tradition even ended. Other than in a church setting, I was not seeing any elders I could entrust.

Throughout many collectivist cultures, such as Native American communities, elders play an elementary role. The elder was appointed to hand down insights, guidance, stories, lessons, and wisdom to the next generations.

I noticed I was living in a society that had more "olders" than it did elders.

In these times, our clergy, counselors, coaches, consultants, and mentors are stepping in to help empower future generations. Thank goodness! When individualistic societies minimize the role of elders passing down wisdom, current and future generations struggle with emotional maturity. I've experienced this first-hand as a woman and mother.

Ken Wilber, considered by many as the father of modern-day Integral Theory, speaks to the difference between growing up and waking up. We all grow up chronologically. Yet to mature in all of our human intelligence centers is completely optional and required if we are to wake up to new potentials.

Growing up, I asked my parents if God was real or not. My mom would say, "Whatever you believe is true." I thought that was a bunch of hogwash. There had to be a truth. From 14 years on, I set out to find the truth about all of reality. No small task. Along my journey into truth, I learned so much about the fabric of reality through quantum physics, the brilliance of the human mind through psychology and spiritual pursuits, and how the energy we put out is the energy that comes back.

Although I learned we live in a society that has more olders than elders, I also discovered how coaching is the new elder on the scene. Coaching steps in to help people optimize their quality of life, their self-understanding, and their capacity to leave the world better than they found it. Yet, it all comes to fruition through the invitation coaching places on the doorstep of people's own wisdom.

You have everything
Figured out,

When you have everything
Figured within.

INDUSTRY CHALLENGES

I became certified as a coach in 2005. I remember when people would ask me what I did for a living, and I would reply, "I am a coach." Then, they would ask, "Oh, interesting. What sport?"

Those days are coming to an end. More and more companies hire professional coaches, people hire personal coaches, and the media is making fun of us. You know your profession has made it when the media starts to make fun of it! I've seen commercials joking, "I need to consult my life coach." Or comics that joke, "My coach had to reschedule; he went on a bender last night!" Yep. That was a comic I ran into one morning.

It is good to be aware of the challenges so you are ready to respond if you run into an issue. Some issues coaches bump up against:

- Confusion with counseling and consulting approaches
- Wild-west of entrepreneurs using the title "coach" without any training and doing other modalities under the umbrella of coaching
- Misunderstandings around what professional coaches do, making marketing services a unique experience (what works in other fields does not always translate to coaches)

It is true, many people still are learning all about the world of coaching. I have decided to take this as an opportunity to educate people and invite them to try it out. Many coaches give a free session so that someone can experience the coaching difference firsthand. If you tell someone, "I believe you have your own answers." They might naturally question, "Um, then why am I not successful yet?"

Many coaches have successfully marketed their services by speaking to the results and benefits of coaching rather than the approach itself, which is harder to grasp until it is experienced.

The experience of coaching
is what illuminates the path.

CREDENTIALLING & STANDARDS

Coaching is a peer-regulated industry and not government-regulated. The government regulates any sector that has the potential to breach ethical boundaries or do harm. Some examples are medicine, psychology, massage, and tax preparation. Coaching, consulting, yoga, and personal training are some examples of peer-regulated professions. In a peer- regulated industry, you have groups of peers who come together to establish standards, ethics, best practices, and credentials that reflect these standards.

Currently, the International Coaching Federation (ICF) is seen as the global standard-setter and was the first group of peers to protect the profession as it grew.

In coaching, there are three components to consider in becoming credentialed.

1. Training: Hours of coach-specific training in coaching competencies.
2. Certification: A training program that evaluates competency proficiency to ensure standards are met.

3. Credentialing: After training, or training and certification, a coach can apply for a professional credential through the ICF.

Please visit the ICF's website to view their current credentialing requirements. https://coachingfederation.org

CHAPTER THREE

℘ Coaching Foundations ℘

Now that you are familiar with the coaching landscape, let's lay a solid foundation to build upon.

In Chapter Three, we will cover all of the foundational underpinnings of coaching so that you can be confident in your coaching and professional representation of coaching. We start by exploring what coaching is, compared to other professional modalities. We then move into the tenets that make coaching such a profoundly unique approach. We will then look at the different styles of coaching and approaches to consider.

Coaching is an art and a science. We will discover how the art shows up and what is entailed in the science of coaching. After that, we explore the four dimensions of masterful coaching and the stages of coaching mastery.

All of these topics are essential components to establishing a solid foundation as a professional coach.

COACHING DISTINCTIONS

Coaching is a completely unique modality. In order to better understand what coaching is, it is helpful to understand what coaching is *not*. Once we cultivate a firm foundational comprehension of what coaching is and isn't, learning how to coach comes much more naturally.

Coaching is so highly unique and specialized that it is often a misunderstood approach.

Most coaches will give a free coaching session because experiencing coaching often yields a more direct understanding of coaching than trying to verbally explain it.

Coaches often report that explaining coaching feels wonky. For example:

> *Potential client: "What is it you do? I think I may need coaching!"*
> *Coach: "I help you find your own answers. I believe you have your best answers."*
> *Potential Client: "If I have my own answers, why am I stuck?"*
> *Coach: "Our answers are sometimes buried within us. I ask you questions to get you to your own answer versus giving advice. As a coach, I see you as whole, fully resourced, and complete."*

In a world where people just want you to tell them what to do, the efficacy of coaching can come across as nebulous. If you haven't yet experienced being coached to your own solutions or the process of diving within to discover new wisdom, it can be hard to grasp the concept. Yet people discover that when they experience being coached, it is rather addicting! On the flip side, people often do not like being told what to do. Being put in touch with your own power is so empowering and feels great. This is why coaching is a great approach for leaders, directors, and teenagers. It invites collaboration and contribution through what I call the "wisdom of we."

Next, we will dive into the three primary helping professions of coaching, consulting, and counseling.

THE THREE C'S

In this segment, we will look at the very clear distinctions between each profession and approach differentials. While there are overlaps of some skills used in each approach, the foundation of each approach is vastly unique, specialized, and well defined.

COACHING

Coaching is unique because it is 100% client-driven. The ICF adheres to a form of coaching that honors the client as the expert of their life and believes that every client is creative, resourceful, and whole.

If clients have all of their answers, and they are creative, resourceful, and whole, then why would they need to hire a coach?

Simply put: We don't always realize our wholeness. We can't always see our best solutions. When you are in the fishbowl, it is hard to see out. Coaching steps in to put a client in touch with their potential, using the vehicle of their own skills, values, beliefs, and wisdom.

Coaching invites subconscious potentials to surface to the conscious. Coaching invites unconscious beliefs, defenses, and conditioned responses into the conscious. Coaching invites a person to come into full alignment with their core values and personal power, so they can lead life confidently.

This process expands a person's capacity to establish and attain goals.

CONSULTING

According to Google definitions, consulting is "The business of giving specialized advice to professionals, typically in financial and business matters."

Consultants are hired when missing information is needed to succeed. Consultants are advisors hired to deliver results. They give direction and provide insights, processes, and information in a specialized area of expertise.

Consultants and advisors are found in areas such as business, technology, education, farming, mechanics, engineering, and health industries.

COUNSELING

Counselors, psychologists, and therapists are trained and licensed mental health providers who diagnose and treat emotional traumas or illnesses.

While some counselors are more coach-like, they are hired to help someone heal aspects of their emotional life. Therapy is excellent when there is a trauma, addiction, or a life problem that has gotten larger than the person can handle without proper guidance.

BREAKING IT ALL DOWN

Below are some key distinctions between each field.

Coaching definition:	Counseling definition:	Consulting definition:
The psychology of human potential. A skill and process that "honors the client as the expert in his/her life and work." - ICF Definition	Diagnosis and treatment of mental illness, imbalance, or instability around life issues.	The business of giving specialized advice to professionals, typically in financial and business matters.

Coaching is best:	Counseling is best:	Consulting is best:
• Client is ready for growth; something is ready to awaken. • Reaching a new potential or goal in life or work. • Empowerment needs to come from within. • Personal and/or professional development. • Client is ready to self-actualize, self-develop, and expand capacity. • Client takes action and is self-responsible, self-generating.	• Treatment for past trauma or abuse. • Emotional healing of past of psychological wounds or triggers. • Diagnosing emotional imbalances or illness. • Problems have become "bigger than" the patient. • Patient needs guidance for handling and healing from problems. • Medical diagnosis.	• Filling information gaps. • Expertise is required. • Technical, business, or health issues needing information to move forward. • Teaching a process is needed.

Coaching focus:	Counseling focus:	Consulting focus:
• Client Growth • Creating future	• Healing • Guidance	• Information • Process

Coaching skills:	Coaching skills:	Coaching skills:
• Program	• Treatment	• Teaching
• Observation	• Diagnosis	• Analyzing
• Reflection	• Guidance	• Reporting
• Inviting	• Connecting Dots	• Strategy
• Socratic Method	• Empathy	• Assessment
• Empathy	• Reflection	• Implementing
• Holding Space	• Observation	• Other: depending on scope
• Somatic Inquiry	• Helping	
• Timing	• Holding Space	
• Intuition	• Intuition	
• Other: depending on scope	• Other: depending on scope	

ADDITIONAL CONSIDERATIONS:

Coaching, like counseling, gets personal. Where are the lines drawn?

I interviewed psychologist Ana Melikian. Ana transitioned from being a psychologist into coaching and offers a clear way to understand the distinctions. She outlines that in therapy, she would help people get from -10 to at least neutral. In coaching, she helps people go from neutral to +10.

Therapy   Coaching

- 10 - 9 - 8 - 7 - 6 - 5 - 4 - 3 - 2 - 1 -0-   VS.   -0- +1 +2 +3 +4 +5 +6 +7 +8 +9 +10

Therapists are trained and licensed to help facilitate healing and navigate self-agency around emotional wounds, traumas, or family matters.

While coaching can be therapeutic, it is not therapy and never replaces therapy or a licensed therapist. It is important to note that any therapeutic experiences do not come from the coach. Sometimes the client may heal something because of the self-discovery process that the coach holds space for.

For example, when I was around four years old, I was irrationally petrified of water. My parents wanted me to have swimming lessons so I could get over my fear. The swim instructor scooped me up into her arms and proceeded to walk me out into deeper waters. She kept telling me, "You are safe. You are safe. Everything is OK." The next thing I knew, I was being thrust underwater and thought I was drowning. It was horrifying!

As an adult in coaching, I later uncovered the unconscious beliefs I took away from that experience. I found I became skeptical about feeling safe in life. I went from believing adults were safe to believing adults were not to be trusted.

Coaching helped me take back parts of myself I didn't realize were off-center because of past experiences I had accumulated and to self-examine my current truths. The self- reflection coaching offered me did help me self-heal my life in those areas.

Therapy helped me heal the wounds that were bigger than me, the ones that needed more than self-reflection, the ones that had deeper roots than coaching could touch.

As coaches, we want to be very clear about our scope of practice and what is outside our scope of practice.

BLENDING MODALITIES

Many of our students come in with a background in some form of advising, counseling, consulting, directing, or teaching. It is possible to blend modalities; however, you will need to be upfront and clear with your client about exactly what your approach entails.

Having clear boundaries creates clarity for the client. Here are some key things to consider if you are potentially blending modalities or have a background as a consultant or counselor:

- A coach with full expertise in an area can be transparent about this with a client and check in about the client's needs. Are they in need of coaching, consulting, or both?
- A coach with some expertise may state within a coaching session, "I'm going to take my coaching hat off for a moment and put on my advising hat." A coach may offer information, then "put the coaching hat back on," and coach the client around their presented information.
- It is a best business practice to state your primary modality in your title. Counselors may use coaching skills to help, but if their primary approach is counseling the person, the title to declare would be "counselor." If your primary approach is coaching, but you occasionally consult in a session, then the primary designation is "coach."
- It is not advisable or ethical to counsel someone who came into a coaching agreement and sought coaching. If you have a counseling background and are a coach, be very clear where your boundaries are and get the training to help you remain neutral as a coach.

BLENDING MODALITIES & BEST PRACTICES

Adding coaching skills to counseling:

Counsel can use coaching skills such as crafting powerful questions, anchoring insights through metaphor, inviting a shift in perspective, and somatic inquiry. Adding coaching to counseling can be a very engaging and empowering approach. When counseling is the prime modality, the counselor has a direction they are helping a client get to that stems from the treatment plan and diagnosis. Coaching skills may enhance the process. The primary difference? A coach does not guide the client or direct the client. The coach 100% follows the client's lead. Counselors are professionally hired to guide the client.

Adding counseling to coaching:

Counseling a client that came for coaching is the equivalent of hijacking the client's agenda. It is never advised to add any counseling to coaching. Adding counseling creates a power differential and confuses the client.

In coaching, we are here to help the client find their power. If I step in and guide or counsel, then I'm taking away their opportunity to self-generate. For example, the power dynamic shifts when therapists leverage their therapy background to preface advice-giving. If advice is given, the client can begin to give their power over to the coach.

If you have a therapy background, you can use your wisdom, knowledge, and experience to help formulate questions. It is best practice not to do formal counseling or guiding to the coaching process.

Adding consulting to coaching:

This one depends! It can be a positive or a negative, depending.

In health and business coaching, missing information needed for success is very common for the client. When I was a personal trainer, I would advise people what to eat, work out safely, and give general health tips.

When I became a health coach, I would fold in the advice if the need arose. It worked well, and I would never assume my advice or information was what the client needed. I would ask questions like, "Does that pertain to you?" "Do you think that approach might be useful?" "Does any of what I said resonate?"

The business coaches I know also do a certain level of advising/consulting and come into the business arena with some expertise. The two can blend well if the coach is transparent that their advice may or may not land for the client and that the priority is to follow the client's needs and coach them to craft their unique success formula.

As a coach, if we are doing any consulting, we need to make sure as a professional coach that when we give a piece of advice with a "take it or leave it attitude." We honor the client when we turn any advice given back over to them, see if it makes sense, and coach them around any implementation.

Every single human being has their own unique success formula. We are not a one size fits all species.

Adding coaching to consulting: ✓
Adding coaching skills to consulting is hands-down powerful!

If you are already a consultant, adding coaching will potentiate your approach. This is because every person, team, relationship, company all have their own unique success formula. If you develop a strategy and give the same strategy to two different companies, one might succeed and the other fail. Why? Each has its own unique default settings, culture, beliefs, values, and approaches.

One of our coaching students that came to add coaching to her thriving consulting practice put it this way: "Coaching is perfect when my client can't hold the consulting."

A coach is trained to meet people exactly where they are at, help them remove blocks to success, and up-level their approaches.

After delivering a strategy, following it up with coaching a client around implementation will ensure more clients will yield even more outstanding results.

IN SUMMARY:
  ✓   People come to counseling for emotional support, guidance, and healing.
  ✓   People come to consulting for missing information.
  ✓   People come to coaching when something within them is ready to awaken, grow, and expand!

THE TENETS OF COACHING

Coaching efficacy is based upon eight fundamental tenets. Each tenant is based on a principle that coaches can stand upon to develop their mastery as a coach.

The coach's goal is to hold space and carry a pure curiosity for the truths buried within each amazing client. These tenets support and empower this aim.

An established coaching relationship creates a transformative container for the client. These tenets invite a potentiated space for the client to grow and expand their potentials.

Let's unpack each of these tenets. Each of them activates possibilities in their own way by elevating the coaching relationship to its fullest.

 # 1 - Each client is whole, complete, resourced, and capable.
What happens if I view my client as fragmented, incomplete, or incapable? My process, and their progress, can be drastically hindered. Viewing and believing in the client's wholeness, resourcefulness, and growing capacities is paramount.

Each human is whole and complete as we are. The problem? We don't feel like it. We can get entangled in illusions and self-limitations that cloud the truth of what we are capable of.

Masterful coaches reflect the client's wholeness, resources fullness, and expanding capacities back to them. You know you have done your job as a coach when the client begins to resourcefully lead their life through their wholeness by engaging all of their expanding capacities.

#2 - The client's wholeness is their internal compass.
Are our wisest answers ever found within our fragmented self? The concept of fragmentation entails breaking off and separating from our true self. Fear fragments us internally from accessing potentials.

What does it mean to relate to life through wholeness and let our wholeness steer us like a compass? It means we live life empowered, engaged, and ready. When we invite our clients to view life through the whole of who they are, this illuminates all of the capacities so that they become integratively aware. Understanding that the client's wholeness is their most empowering compass is key to masterful coaching.

#3 – Each client carries within them their own unique success formula.
One size does not fit all!

What works for one client may fall completely flat for another. What worked for me may not work for you. Even how I skillfully meditate may be different than how you might approach mediation.

We can follow best practices and success principles, but how I approach anything will be unique to me, and how you approach anything will be unique. For example, when observing a coaching session, we see that what I see as avenues to take in a session will differ from the avenues you take. Diversity of choice is the beauty of life.

As a coach, it is wise to note that we can be the expert of something in the external world; however, we will never be an expert in someone else's inner world, internal workings, or internal makeup. This tenet is why coaching exists. Our job as a coach is to help our clients understand and formulate their unique success formula in their life according to their gifts, values, and desired outcomes.

Understanding this tenet is how we honor the client and how they honor themselves.

#4 – The client's wisdom is their most valuable asset.
When we are in a problem, where is the solution? The solution is waiting to be found. If the solution were already present, then there wouldn't be a problem. Within the client is where solutions surface. Truths are often hidden, and it is the coach's role to help the client excavate their truth.

Having a human mind can be an empowering experience or feel fragmented. This is because, as human beings, we are capable of self-deception. The problem with self- deception is that it is hard to catch and covers up our deeper inner knowing.

Inner knowing illuminates a client's wisdom. As we help our clients access their inner knowing, they begin to start growing. As a coach, you know a session is impactful when the client leaves a session glowing because their wisdom is showing.

Masterful coaches reflect the client's wisdom back to them and understand that wisdom is the client's most valuable asset to living a potentiated life.

#5 - *True perceptions expand into potentials.*
What happens when we have a false perception? It blocks us from what is possible. Understanding the powerful role of perception in a client's life is fundamental to masterful and transformational coaching.

Helping our clients see clearly is fundamental to avoiding self-limiting beliefs and stepping into their truth. Helping our clients see clearly is how we help our clients access the highest aspects of themselves.

Masterful coaches understand the power of perception and help their clients navigate beyond illusions and into truth.

#6 - *Masterful coaching is a melding of the client's and coach's wisdom.*
Is coaching about the client's wisdom? Yes. Is coaching about the coach's wisdom? Yes. Masterful coaching interweaves the wisdom of both parties. Masterful coaching is a dance, a relationship, a partnering for new potentials.

Masterful coaches do not leave their wisdom at the door; they understand when, why, and how to fold in their wisdom for the client's empowerment. Masterful coaches know that we reach our human potential when we are in relationship.

#7 - Heart-centered presence is an activating agent to what is possible.
If I am worried about what I'm going to ask my client next, where am I? I am no longer with my client. I am no longer present to their needs, their subtle cues, their nuances. When I am sitting in my head, I've left the client and focused on me.

Coaching presence is the container for transformational coaching. A heart-centered presence is even more potent. The energy the coach brings into the session impacts the client. In a relationship, we are connected. When I embody a heart-centered presence, I invite the client into their heart, where their truth is illuminated.

In coaching, we hold space.

In masterful coaching, we hold a potentiated space.

#8 – Coaching perfection does not exist. Masterful coaching does.
I have good news and bad news. Bad news first. You will never be a perfect coach. Being perfect, asking the perfect questions 100% of the time, and always knowing exactly what to ask or say next is not probable. I am so sorry.

Now the good news. The good news is that you will never be a perfect coach. Coaching is not about being perfect. Hurray! Can you find the relief in not having to be perfect? Instead of focusing on perfection, focus on presence.

Instead of focusing on the perfect question, listen until the powerful questions pop up organically. Masterful coaching is never about perfection. In masterful coaching, even the imperfectly asked questions serve. Masterful coaching generates from our ability to be responsive, pivot with the client, and stay with the client at each turn.

IN SUMMARY:
1. *Each client is whole, complete, resourced, and capable.*
2. *The client's wholeness is their internal compass.*

3. *Each client carries within them their own unique success formula.*

4. *The client's wisdom is their most valuable asset.*

5. *True perceptions expand into potentials.*

6. *Masterful coaching is a melding of the client's and coach's wisdom.*

7. *Heart-centered presence is an activating agent to what is possible.*

8. *Coaching perfection does not exist. Masterful coaching does.*

COACHING EFFICACY

Coaches are hired to help leaders, professionals, groups, couples, or individuals potentiate and integrate into their potential.

In coaching, people:
- Connect to their values
- Grow in their emotional intelligence
- Build upon natural strengths and gifts
- Expand in their capacities
- Set and attain goals

Human beings are in a unique position.

We have the power of sentience. We are capable of abstract thought. We grasp intricate philosophies, pilot spaceships, create art, build skyscrapers and water parks. We are capable of spiritual depth, experience intimacy, have an imagination and free will... just to name just a few.

Once I was walking down a San Diego street on the way to the beach with my husband. To my left was a giant fig tree! What was so special about this? Well, at home, I had a fig tree. I kept it indoors, away from the scorching Tucson heat, and it was about six feet tall.

This tree in San Diego had to be at least thirty to forty feet and was so lush with leaves I couldn't see through it to the other side. My tree? Well, let's just say I placed it in front of a window, and I could still see out of the window no problem.

What was the difference?

The San Diego tree was in its element! The conditions were just right for it to skyrocket to its fullest potential.

My tree? Well, it was potted for one. I did water it, but the desert air is very dry. I also sprayed it with a water bottle, but that's not even close to mimicking the moist beach air.

Plants do not have a choice. If they don't have an environment that supports them, they don't do well. When they are in their element and have all of their needs met, they thrive.

People do have a choice. We are our own soil, nourishment, air, and nutrients. What we put in our minds, hearts, and bodies is our call. We can get our needs met. Yes, external factors impact us, but we have response choices.

Plants are a part of life. Life replicates and responds.

People are a part of life and consciousness. Consciousness responds and chooses. Consciousness is aware.

Our consciousness, our humanity, is the arena of human potential that coaching engages.

Logical or Emotional Efficacy?

Which part of the brain lends to action and learning? Logical or emotional?

A study cited by the ICF talks about the brain and coaching. When someone was given advice, it lit up the logical part of the brain, and there wasn't ownership of the information taken in. Answering questions engaged both the logical and emotional parts of the brain. The emotional part of the brain is linked to inspiration, action, and ownership. (7)

Coaching engages the whole brain, which elevates the client's capacities. If we show someone the way, there is much less ownership.

When someone is intrinsically motivated, follow-through is more natural and inspired. External motivations only go so far and require much more forced energy or willpower. Willpower only gets us so far.

Integrative coaching is so effective because it engages the whole brain and the whole person: somatically, neurologically, mentally, and emotionally. Engaging a client through the wholeness of their capacity yields profound results.

Coaching that only engages thinking can only get so far. In this manual, you will learn the power of coaching the whole person and coaching the wholeness of the person. We travel beyond the mind to help the client gain access to a broader range of possibilities.

Next, let's look at the coaching approaches and styles to be aware of.

COACHING APPROACHES

There are two primary coaching approaches. The first is transactional. The second is transformational.

TRANSACTIONAL COACHING:
- Logistical: When, where, what, how, who
- Logical
- Actions and results
- Measurable

TRANSFORMATIONAL COACHING:
- Why? Motive?
- Beneath the surface
- Relationship to
- Belief examining

- Perspective shifting Masterful coaches engage both. Why not just go for transformation?

If a client has an amazing, mind-blowing epiphany during a session and then goes home feeling happy, but nothing changes in their approach to life, where does that epiphany live? In the land of thought and theory.

To bring the theory to life requires action and follow-through. After a client shifts, following up with the logistics of:
- What actions do you want to take around this?
- What could get in the way? How do you want to handle obstacles?
- When do you want to do this by?
- What accountability or resources do you need?

Transformational is where "awesome" comes from. Transactional brings "awesome" to life!

COACHING STYLES

"Why would you not take this public speaking opportunity?!" I was sitting next to a coach at a networking event.

The coach I sat next to that day offered me a challenge question. I had an opportunity to speak at a large convention. I was about to bow out. She pushed me to reconsider. I could tell she wanted me to take this opportunity and not pass it up. Those who know me know I'm a mega introvert. On the introvert scale of one to ten, ten being the most, I am a ten. To speak to a large audience had zero appeal to me. I'd rather spend my energy coaching, writing, and reading. Her challenge came across as a judgment to me, though. I know she wanted to help me reach my potential, yet I didn't want to feel pushed or challenged in that direction just yet. I had other areas I wanted to be pushed in.

Then I met Karen. Her coaching approach was music to my ears. She said, "If you don't resonate with speaking, have you considered writing?" I loved to write! Yes, this open, curious coaching style was much more aligned and helpful for me at that time.

Then other times in my life when I needed more push, challenge, and to be called out on my blind spots, I would go to Sandy. Sandy was a powerhouse and a velvet hammer. She had a way of lasering in to the gaps and empathetically helping you close them. Many sessions with Sandy resulted in tears. Tears of realization. Tears of growing pains. Tears of joy.

No one coaching style is good or bad, right or wrong. Each serves a purpose and serves people needing that style.

Styles of coaching are better thought of on a spectrum.

Passive ☒　　　　　　→ Assertive

Each coach has their own style that will be perfect for the clients they wish to serve. Masterful coaches develop the capacity to shift their style according to the need of the client.

Sometimes a client may need us to be more passive, and other times they may need us to deliver a kick-in-the-pants challenge. That is the art of coaching: sensing when to shift in support of the client.

In my experience, most coaches have a default setting. I default to passive as an introvert, whereas my mentor Sandy was more extroverted and assertive. She often and admittedly overstepped. I've also seen introverted coaches take a more assertive approach. There is no one formula when it comes to forming your coaching style.

I want to save you years of struggle by inviting you to step into the unique style that is authentic to you and then master the art of adaptation and responsiveness to meet the shifting needs of your clients.

I once attended a workshop by Mary Morrisey, a respected speaker and coach. She told the story of a retreat she attended where the Dali Lama spoke.

The following day she attended a group discussion, and the woman next to her asked Mary a question. Mary recalled what the Dali Lama taught and answered the woman's question based on her recollection. The woman had a complete epiphany from what Mary shared! Mary told her she just repeated what the Dali Lama said. The woman responded by sharing that she understood he said it, but the way Mary said it helped the dots connect for her in a completely new way.

This is how it is with our clients. Our clients need us to be our genuine self. They need us to be present to our gifts so that we can gift them with the present of theirs.

THE ART & SCIENCE OF POSSIBILITY
Get this!

We do not create possibilities. Possibilities already exist within each of us. Possibilities exist twenty-four hours a day, seven days a week, and 365 days a year.

The question is: Do we have access to the possibilities within us?

The more we develop our capacities, the more access we gain. The more reactive, closed, and unwilling, the less access we have.

For example, if I'm reactive at work, what is the probability of getting a promotion? Little to none; however, if I learn how to put aside my reactivity, listen to my co-workers in new ways and ask questions that inspire people, how likely am I to get a promotion? I would at least have a chance. I've gained access.

Coaching is both an *art* and science of gaining access to possibilities.

As coaches, we help our clients identify the blockages and create new openings. Openings then lead to opportunities. Some opportunities we create for ourselves and others we walk into.

"Luck is what happens when
preparation meets opportunity."
~ Seneca, Roman philosopher

COACHING IS AN ART

Coaching delves into the abstractions and intangible arenas of human potential. We are capable of intuition, envisioning, mindsets, emotional depth, belief questioning, accessing the highest self, and awareness of the egoic self.

To the masterful coach, coaching is the art of adapting to the depths and abstractions. We are dancing around in the world of possibilities with our clients and fishing for openings. We are inviting new outcomes and evoking new visions. We are ninjas at tuning in to what is not being said and hearing our clients intuitively.

COACHING IS A SCIENCE

Coaching is results-based. Action-oriented. Tangible, measurable. Coaching includes models, framing, methodology, and offers client assessment tools.

Masterful coaches help their clients examine their mental equations. How will I feel if I equate my self-worth to my income and lose a significant commission? If I equate my self- worth to my innate gifts and I'm living out of those gifts, how will I feel? Coaching is both an art and a science. Coaching is both backward and forwards. It is backward because, in coaching, we begin with the end in mind. "Where do you want to be in 10 years?" "Who do you want to be?" "What wants to be done differently?" In coaching, we then reverse- engineer to move forwards. "What actions are next?" "Where are you aligned with your value of self-trust?" Coaching is very Taoist in concept. To lead our clients to their potential, we must follow them to their truth.

COACHING AS A NEUROSCIENCE

Any time we grow and stretch in new ways, we are creating new habits. New habits form neuropathways in the brain. In personal training, I learned that it takes twelve weeks to develop a new neuropathway; we call this a habit.

Many coaches require a client to complete a minimum of a three- to six-month program because new behaviors are being formed. It takes time to go from planting the seeds of ideas to expanding its roots and growing new fruits. Growth is a process.

You will learn how to pull together a high-impact coaching program in the chapter Coaching Program Frameworks.

The brilliant thing about coaching is that the learning, the new skills, and the expanded capacities all go with us for a lifetime. Once those new neuropathways are formed, they are there, like learning to ride a bike.

*Coaching is a short-term investment
with life-long positive impact!*

THE FOUR DIMENSIONS OF MASTERFUL COACHING

My oldest son Alec came back to visit from college. He challenged his younger brother Ashton to a game of chess. Ashton didn't want to play chess with Alec because Alec always won. Alec wouldn't let up. We all harped on Alec about pressuring his brother. We then joked about how nobody enjoyed playing chess with Alec because losing isn't fun.

Alec responded, "But, I don't know how to play chess." We all burst out laughing. He said, "No, really. I'm not joking. I know a few moves to win. I don't actually know the art of playing chess. Without those formulas, I would lose every time."

After seeing "The Queen's Gambit," the Netflix series about a genius chess player, I now see what he was saying. Truly knowing how to play chess masterfully is an organic and intuitive process. If you only know the formulas and play someone who knows one more formula than you, you lose; however, the science can get you far until you master the art.

I remember watching a complete coaching transformation happen in under ten minutes when I was new to coaching. I remember wishing I could be that good and didn't understand how masterful coaches could work their magic and voilà! My investigative side set out immediately to unearth what was going on in the background that allowed these coaches to work such magic. It seemed like an impossible task, but I had to see if there was some formula to it!

I asked three questions:
1. What is the makeup of a masterful coach?
2. How do masterful coaches work their magic?
3. Can I yield the same results, or do you have to be born with the gift?

I found that there are four dimensions that masterful coaches enter into to help their clients yield profound transformations.

These are best understood in the physical plane first.

If you look up, there is above.
Look down, there a below.
There is what is in front of you.
There is what is behind you.

Spiritual and psychologically speaking, these physical dimensions are also brilliant correlations to the four dimensions of masterful coaching.

Above is a bigger picture. Below are roots.
In front is a future. Behind is a past.

ABOVE

Masterful coaches invite a bigger picture.

How easy is it to read a label from inside the jar?

When we are stuck in a problem, we cannot readily see outside of the problem. How easy is it to read a label from inside the jar? To see outside of a problem, we must be outside of the problem. We step out of it by taking a bigger picture view. Taking a big picture view helps us rise above and hold an expanding perspective while facing an issue.

Masterful coaches take their clients to the big picture of their lives. What is their bigger picture? Masterful coaches include the client's values, gifts, callings, end goals, and superpowers. These ingredients activate a broader range of possibilities.

When the client's view is no longer limited or constricted, they shift to expansive, inclusive, and open options. This view helps a client consider all parts. The client has an opportunity to become a big-picture problem-solver and begin to think in more integratively intelligent ways.

Additionally, as the coach, we do not join the client in the problem when we maintain a bigger picture perspective. We maintain neutrality by remaining above the issue.

To coach from a bigger picture, remember:
- This too shall pass.
- The relationship to the issue matters more than the issue itself.
- This client has superpowers and can rise above this.
- This client carries the answer to this and all issues.

At least once in every coaching session, I invite you to take your client to visit their bigger picture. Staying put in the problem with a client, we miss the whole point of coaching.

Coaching is about rising above, expanding, and seeing farther. A few examples of taking a client to a bigger picture:
- What if you were on the top of a mountain looking down at this problem. What do you see is possible from above?

- If you were a hawk flying above, what do you see?
- What happens if you rose above this?

BELOW

Masterful coaches see beneath the surface. They invite the client to understand the roots of an issue so that they can create new fruits. Let's unpack this.

Masterful coaches know that powerful questions are formed by listening beneath the words to locate what is not being said. The root of an issue is beneath the surface. Getting to the roots transforms the fruits.

In masterful coaching, we take the client deeper, down to the roots. When we take a client to the sources, this helps the client change course.

Below the surface, we can take pause.
Below the surface, we find the cause.
Below the surface, we get to the heart.
Below the surface, we can choose a brand-new start.

The roots of an issue represent the client's underlying beliefs. There are supportive or positive beliefs. Let's call these seeds. Then there are negative or limiting beliefs. Let's call these weeds. When a client fosters a new idea, this is like a freshly planted seed. Seeds place the client at the level of cause. Weeds, on the other hand, truncate fruitful outcomes. Weeds are living at the level of effect.

Masterful coaches take the client beneath the surface to help them examine: 1) Are there any beliefs constricting or limiting them like overgrown weeds? 2) What are the seeds of positive new beliefs?

As a coach, we can take a client to pull any weeds and plant new seeds! All of this is possible once we invite our client to look beneath the surface.

A Course in Miracle shares with us that, "We are never upset for the reasons we think." Go to the roots.

IN-FRONT

What is in front of a client? Their future. The question is, what type of future is the client seeing? What the client sees is important because how they are seeing leads to how they are being.

Let's unpack this.

Past experiences craft our assumptions, judgments, and generalizations. Positive or negative. Conscious or unconscious. Human beings are capable of abstract thought. Abstract thought has the potential to be a blessing, curse, asset, or liability.

How we use this intelligence either binds us or frees us. Having an abstract mind gives us the ability to create a projection. A projection is an aspect of the human imagination, where we imagine the future. We can live through two types of projections.

A storyline is the first type of projection and is a critical distinction to understand as a coach. Stories are crafted based on our past experiences or fears of what we don't want. Stories we tell ourselves about our life include our defenses, triumphs, and our beliefs about who or what we are. Stories are an effect because they are based on the past. Stories are crafty.

We can tell ourselves we are better than, less than, and anything in between. We can equate our self-worth to external factors in the land of story. We can look like the victor or the victim in the tales we tell ourselves and others.

Our stories lines keep the past engaged and alive in the mind's eye. Stories are how the past shows up in our future. Masterful coaches invite their clients to self-examine: Is what you are running from defining what you are running to?

When our past shows up in our future, we see patterned ways of being that become predictable and self-fulfilling. Can you recall someone you can't say a certain thing around because the reaction is predictable?

It is narratives from the past that keep us anchored, and these anchors limit human potential. What happens when we release the anchors and step out of a story? What happens when the narrative isn't based upon what was or what is? What happens when we step out of the effect and into the cause?

Peter Drucker says:

*"The best way to predict
the future is to create it."*

The other form of projection we are capable of is called vision. Vision is different from a storyline. Vision begins with the end in mind. Vision engages new possibilities within us and is a catalyst for something greater. Projections from the past are binding, while vision carries the silver lining.

Masterful coaches help clients step out of projections that stem from their protections and into a bigger vision that is mission-driven. Masterful coaches help the client identify what projection the client is living through, placing them at the cause of their life.

BEHIND
What is behind a client? Their past.

The question is, what type of past is the client seeing? Again, how they are seeing leads to how they are being. Let's unpack this.

How we relate to the past is how we relate to our future. Interpretations of the past inform our assumptions, judgments, beliefs, fears, and generalizations in the present. Consciously or unconsciously.

For example:
1. An event that happens.
2. The brain determines if that event was safe or unsafe.
3. We equate unsafe to bad and safe with good.
4. We project similar events will be the same.

Human beings, however, don't typically stop at what happened. Humans default to creating a story around what happened. When we generate a story around what happened, it becomes like fodder for our fears. We then can create beliefs around our stories. Before we know it, we are living with false beliefs without even knowing it. These are anchored in beneath us as we do life.

The past can interfere with our clarity of the future until we become aware. Masterful coaches invite new awareness so the client can shed interpretations, assumptions, and limitations that keep them anchored to the past. Masterful coaches also help their clients use past experiences to inform their future. They understand that past experiences offer a contrast to help us determine what we want and don't want to show up in our future. In this regard, masterful coaches help clients use the past as stepping stones to a brighter future.

IN SUMMARY

Masterful coaches understand how all four dimensions potentiate the coaching experience.

Masterful coaches understand each dimension has its illusions and truths, traps, and freedoms. They see how the client's treasure of truth is beneath the illusion waiting to be discovered, excavated, and curated. To masterfully coach your client, I invite you to learn how to journey to all four dimensions so that they can live a life empowered by the clarity of their own vision.

I also invite you to honor the stages of your mastery as your potential unfolds.

HONORING THE STAGES OF MASTERY

Coaching is a highly unique approach. My personal experience and the majority of students I work with report that learning to coach feels counterintuitive and very awkward…at first. It makes sense. We want to help. We want to be the savior. We want the client to get results. And to do that I'm being asked to show up as a blank slate and not advise?! Scary.

I also came across an article covering research on how the brain is wired to give advice and find solutions. It makes sense then that learning coaching, learning not to provide answers, feels counterintuitive.

Coaching involves learning to live in the moment, swim in a potentiated space, and navigate through probability and possibility without having answers.

Coaching is ironic.

I have to step into uncertainty to help my client find clarity? I have to lead my client by following them?

I have to remove judgment and trust in the unknown?

Yes! In these spaces of unknowing, the knowing begins growing and glowing! This space is where the transformations happen.

Learning not to provide direction is straightforward yet not easy.

In the first coach training I attended, the instructor threw us into the deep end by requiring us to coach in front of a group of twenty, knowing full well we didn't know how to coach. We were supposed to "figure it out" by trial and error. When we veered from coaching, we got called out. Not helpful.

Another training I attended taught zero coaching skills, we read over competencies, and then everyone was left to figure out what they were doing and how to do it. Not helpful.

I believe in the power of phasing. We first get a feel for the bike with training wheels, then maybe our parents' hands on the handlebars, then eventually we are freewheeling. Then some of us learn how to pop-wheelies.

We move from unconscious incompetence to conscious competency.

→ Unconscious Incompetence
    → Conscious Incompetence
        → Unconscious Competence
            → Conscious Competence!

These stages can be used as valuable focal points to help you progress in your mastery. They are ways to take attainable action steps and not feel confused or wondering if you are on the right track.

STAGE ONE: Framing

Give yourself three to six months in Stage One. This phase we want to understand the Give yourself three to six months in Stage One. In this phase, we gain the fundamentals of effective coaching and begin practicing the framework.

Focal Points:
- Practice: Two or more sessions a month.
- Notice when you are 100% clear on the agenda "takeaway" before proceeding into the body of the session.
- Practice open questions that invite the client to explore.
- Practice reflecting observations and client language.
- Practice calling time and delivering the well-rounded wrap-up.

STAGE TWO: Expanding

Give yourself three to six months in Stage Two. After you are more comfortable with the framework of impactful sessions, it is time to hone your skills further and do some fine-tuning.

Focal Points - Keep doing everything in phase one, plus:
- Practice: Two or more sessions a month.
- Notice when the client has a shift, big or small.
- Practice diving into action directly after a shift happens.
- Practice one question at a time.
- Practice listening deeper.
- End on time.

STAGE THREE: Embodying

Give yourself three to six months in Stage Three. At this stage, we begin to practice listening beneath the surface, picking up more on what is not said, and delivering a well-rounded session. We become more adaptive and masterfully responsive.

Focal Points – Continue what you have learned and add:
- Practice: Two or more sessions a month.
- Questions are open-ended.
- Practice concise delivery.
- Practice listening beneath the surface.
- Invite a bigger picture.
- Get mentor coaching.
- Course correct any patterns or tendencies.

STAGE FOUR: Growing

Stage Four is post-training and certification. Give yourself three to five years in Stage Four. This is being a professional coach and growing in your practice.
- Focus on honing who you are as a coach (outside of session too).
- Embody your brand as a coach.

Focal Points:
- Coaching supervision
- Coaching community and networking

Resources:
- School alumni
- Continuing Education Classes (CCE)
- ICF State Chapter Membership
- ICF Global Membership / Credentialing

STAGE FIVE: Mastering

Stage five is about studying MCC level skill sets and approaches. This can be years or decades in the making.
- Open sessions
- Expanding awareness

Focal Points:
- MCC level training
- MCC mentor coaching

Resources:
- MCC Mentor Coach

ADDITIONAL REFLECTIONS

Coaching is a journey, not a destination.

Coaching is not just a skill set and traverses beyond a profession. Coaching is a way of being and a way of life. A way to honor others, see a brighter future and create brilliant outcomes through the wisdom of we.

Some coaches get training and successfully launch a practice before training is over. The coaches I've seen succeed quickly typically have a marketing, sales, or business ownership background. Other coaches take a few years to get our coaching feet and establish marketing ourselves for the first time. We don't earn a master's degree overnight. Part of the "training" is to practice in the real world. We all launch at different times.

Resist the urge to judge your journey with coaching. A friend of mine once said, "The shortest distance to your goal isn't always a straight line." It is helpful to develop self-acceptance and have compassion for your unique process.

My Journey

My journey with coaching was a classic example of how the path to a private practice isn't always straightforward. I was first trained and certified in 2005. At that point I created a part- time health coaching practice while being a stay-at-home mom part-time. I remained part- time as I completed my degree through 2008.

Around 2009 I went through a divorce. I had to take on a full-time job. I decided to coach both at my new job and on the side. In 2011 I decided to quit my full-time job but didn't have full-time clientele yet, so I sold handmade tile art at local farmer's markets to make ends meet while I grew my private coaching practice back up.

As you can see, not all success is straightforward! Whatever your journey, keep going, and you will get there. Have compassion and acceptance for your unique journey. Even when it doesn't feel like it is coming fast enough, remember success on the way. Laotzu, a Chinese philosopher, reminds us that:

"The journey of a thousand miles
begins with a single step."

CHAPTER FOUR

ཀྵ Mastering Coaching Fundamentals ཀྵ

Now that you have a solid foundation in coaching fundamentals let's start building the frameworks for mastery. Chapter Three helps you build mastery so you can deliver a high- impact coaching session, avoiding hijacking the agenda, and gain clarity around referring out.

We will also explore the fundamental skills, locate and address discrepancies and listen for what is not said.

We then wrap up our fundamentals lessons with a segment on framing new learning for the client to help engage their self-development.

Let's dive in!

THE ANATOMY OF IMPACT
In an impactful coaching session, you will find six key elements. These elements are the anatomy of a high-impact coaching session. I call these the six As.

These six components are:
1. Establishing the **Agenda**
2. Locating **Avenues** of Opportunity

3. Inviting the **Ah-Ha** Moment

4. **Acknowledging** the Client's Truth

5. Moving into **Action**

6. Providing Time for *Assessment*

Let's unpack each of these. Each component is essential to high-impact coaching and has its own timing and structure to consider.

1. Agenda = Priority? Working on? Walk away with?

In coaching, the client is in charge of setting the agenda for the session. In a high-impact session, the agenda includes the client's top priority and the destination they wish to end up at. Without a clearly defined agenda, the conversation can go in circles.

There are many components to taking a well-rounded approach to agenda-setting.

- What would be meaningful to focus on today?
- Is there anything else going on?
- What brings this to the top of the priority list today?
- What would be helpful to walk away with today around this?
- What needs resolved?
- I'm hearing…(reflect back). Did I capture everything?
- Confirmed. Where would you like to begin?

Let's unpack the significance of each of these.

What would be meaningful to focus on?
  o   This is the overall "topic" of the session.

Is there anything else going on that could be a higher priority?
  o   This is a checkpoint question. Double-check if there is anything else going on that needs more attention than what was presented. If we take the first offer at face value, we can miss valuable opportunities. If a client has an issue in the back of their mind while in session,

they could be distracted or antsy the entire time. Sometimes the more pressing items come out towards the end. When we provide space for full exploration, the "hot button" tends to surface.

What makes this topic a priority?

- o Knowing "why" this topic is important and relevant to the Client is helpful to coach them around their agenda in more profound ways.
- o Understanding relevance can help you form powerful questions around the relationship to the issue.

What is the desired takeaway by the end of the session?

- o Understanding the destination helps you keep the client on track and head in the desired direction. If the session gets off track, having a clear goal and destination is valuable to circle back to.

What needs to be resolved around this?

- o What does the Client see are the key issues or obstacles getting in the way? What needs overcome? Exploring these questions helps the session focus on what is most pressing.

Where does the client want to start?

- o The moment you are 100% clear on the goal, the destination, the why, the what (needs resolved), then it is time to dive into the body of the session.
- o Asking the client where they would like to begin is highly efficient. The client already knows what they have already tried and where the "hot button" is.
- o oInviting the client to co-create the session also empowers your client to take the driver's seat.

Notice how a comprehensive, well-established exploration of the agenda sets up the session for greater depth and success.

Mastery Tip #1: *A well-rounded agenda is established through exploration.*

A masterful, well-rounded agenda exploration does not take the original topic at face value. In masterful coaching, we need context.

A masterful opening includes transactional (data collection and measurable take-away) and transformational (contextual) elements.

Mastery Tip #2: *Masterful coaching puts the direction of the session in the hands of the client first.*

When the coach chooses the direction, we can accidentally miss opportunities to laser right in. Or we may accidentally override the client's needs. The client is intimately familiar with the issue they are facing. Asking the client where to begin will take the coaching session straight into the heart of the matter.

Rule of thumb: Step in with options, or session direction, if the client identifies they are unsure where to begin.

Mastery Tip #3: *A well-rounded agenda exploration saves time.*

When first starting as a coach, it is normal to feel like a full exploration of the agenda is wasted time. It seems counterintuitive to spend ten to fifteen minutes exploring when you could be helping the client get results. Don't be fooled by this assumption. A well-rounded exploration of the agenda sets the session up for success and saves time.

Mastery Tip #4: *Let the powerful questions come later.*

When exploring the agenda, resist the urge to start coaching or ask questions that belong in the body of the session.

As a mentor coach listening to session recordings, I sometimes hear powerful questions show up in the agenda-setting part of the session. For example: "When you say upset, tell me more. What does upset means to you?" Before the agenda is established, you may be switching directions, and "upset" may or may not be applicable to the session goals.

Save your powerful questions for the body of the session and place your energy on fully establishing a solid agenda before proceeding.

What do I do if the client doesn't know what they want to work on?

Here are a few things to consider if the client shows up and is unsure what is the most important thing to work on. Consider the reason.

CASE STUDY: "All is well!"

Joe showed up to his session five months into his program, reports all is great and doesn't know what to work on. He had accomplished many goals that he came into coaching for, and things were going well.

At this point, we explored other areas of his life: home life, self-care, health, etcetera. Those areas were all good.

We decided to do a progress review. We reviewed past sessions and themes. As we did, he recognized a looming fear that had gone unaddressed. Suddenly, we had fodder for one of the most profound mindset shifts he was unconsciously needing.

When a client shows up unsure and has been working with you for a while, you can go big picture with a life review or session progress review. These two approaches tend to generate many ideas of what to focus on next. It could also indicate that the client might be ready to graduate from their program. We graduate the client when they feel complete in all ways.

CASE STUDY: "I'm not sure."

Kendra showed up to her second session unsure what to work on. She was so new to coaching that setting the agenda felt daunting, and she was accustomed to counseling where the counselor would take the reins.

When a client is learning how to get the most from coaching, there are a few ways we can help them.

#1 – Session Prep: A prep form can be sent in advance and helps the client consider what they want to accomplish in advance. If you hadn't sent one yet, you could start the session with the questions included in the form.

Typical session prep questions (adapt as needed):
- What have you accomplished since we met last?
- Did any obstacles arise?
- What is the goal for our next session?

#2 – Life exploration: "How is home life?" "How is health?" "Kids?"

#3 – Assessment: We will cover ample tools and assessments. You can offer an assessment that the client can reflect on. Assessments offer opportunities that swiftly locate areas to focus on.

All of these approaches are vital ingredients for transformational sessions. Some of the best sessions come after the client shows up unsure what to work on. It is helpful to remember that it is the coach's responsibility to help the client learn how to be a client and how to get the most from the coaching. Assisting the client in exploring their agenda and prep for a session are two ways we can accomplish this. Once the agenda is fully explored and solidified, then it is time to dive into the body of the session.

So, where shall we begin once the agenda is crystal as a creek?

2. Avenues = Pathways towards the client's destination.

When it is time to dive into the body of the session, we start to take "avenues" to get the client to their goal for the day. There are many paths to the top of the same mountain. As mentioned previously, it is most effective first to ask the client where they want to begin. This allows the session to go right to any hot spots!

Next, we follow the client down avenues leading to the desired take-away. We may offer:

- Factual observations for client reflection (words, options, metaphors)
- Powerful questions that invite a shift in perspective
- Powerful questions that invite self-awareness and learning
- Explorations that contribute to client thinking
- Options for the client to choose the direction of the session
- Challenge to any assumptions or discrepancies

The avenues taken towards the solution entail the art of coaching. We will explore the coaching skills that bring the session to life in greater detail in subsequent chapters.

For now, know that the focus is on observing, inviting, and listening for any shifts or "ah-ha" moments. The "ah-ha" moments happen when the client shifts from problem to solution.

MASTERY TIP: Anytime we dive into solutions and actions before the client has had a shift, the results tend to fall flat. If you notice the client is defensive when you offer a solution, check to see if you dove into actions too soon. Inversely, they might go straight for the actions and overlook the actual underlying issue or cause. Invite the shift! Then dive into action.

3. Ah-ha = Follow the "yes."
Sometimes a client has a huge breakthrough or epiphany. These are obvious because the client calls it out and there is an overt sense of excitement, thrill, or "wow" factor. Blatant "ah-ha" moments are easy. As soon as we spot them, we can then swiftly move to #4 and #5. Acknowledge and celebrate with the client and then move immediately into action.

It is the subtle "ah-ha" that is harder to catch.

Masterful coaches tune in to their clients and do not just wait for the big "wow" moments. Masterful coaches understand that sometimes the subtle "yes" can lead to a bigger "YES."

An ah-ha moment occurs anytime the client stands in their "yes," their inner-knowing, or their truth.

Sometimes they are as subtle as, "Oh." The tone drops in, the grip on the problem loosens, and the client becomes more grounded.

THE SUBTLE "Ah-Ha":
- o Client's tone shifts from lower to higher.
- o Client's tone shifts from higher to lower.
- o Client comments: "Ah." "Hmmm." "I like that." "That I can do."
- o Client's eyes open wider.
- o Client becomes open to more ideas.
- o Client overtly states their truth as a matter of fact without missing a beat.

Catching subtle ah-has takes practice. It takes getting to know your client. It helps you hone and craft your own mastery.

The subtle ah-has are the most important. Here is why:

INVITE MORE:
If you hear a potential shift, the next step is to stop and check it out. Inquire about it. "What was behind the 'Oh' just now?" "What about that do you like?" "I just heard you state a solution and you didn't even bat an eyelash. What do you think about that?"

Inquire about what you are observing. See if it is accurate. If it is an actual opening to a shift, follow it; the shift is typically right around the corner!

If it isn't, that is OK too; sometimes we are close, but the client dives back into something that needs to be resolved. Trust the client and be of service to them. Remember, the goal is to help the client remove the blocks to their success.

NOTE: It is critical to reflect shifts. Sometimes the client does not realize they had a shift and will stay in the problem unless we point the shift out. Reflecting a shift creates an opening for the client, inviting them into the land of solutions.

Once we reflect and confirm a shift, move on to #4.

4. Acknowledge = Confirm and celebrate the "yes."
Once a client has had a shift, celebrate with them! Confirm it. Acknowledge it. Then move to #5, action-taking.

Right now, we are talking about session progression and what lends to a session being effective versus falling flat or going in circles. When it comes to inviting the client forward, we want to follow up any "yes" with an immediate acknowledgment and then swiftly move to #5, the invitation into action.

NOTE: Acknowledgement is also a skill that we want to use throughout a session as well.

5. Action = What steps towards "yes"?
What brings insight to life? Action!

There is energy in the client having a shift. Once you acknowledge the shift, ask:
- "What would you like to do about this?"
- "Now you have identified a, b and c, what are your next steps?"
- "How will you bring this to life?"

An idea is just an idea until it is brought to life! Transformations are anchored in when we transaction them into being.

Consider these spiritual perspectives from A Course in Miracles on bringing new ideas to life:

"You can enslave a body, but an idea is free,
incapable of being kept in prison or limited in any way
except by the mind that thought it."
"If you share a physical possession, you do divide its ownership.
If you share an idea, however, you do not lessen it."
Ideas are meant to expand.

6. Assessment = What is confirmed? Learned? Needed?

To wrap up a session effectively, we want to give the wrap-up its own space. A well- rounded wrap-up includes inviting the client to do a full assessment and connect the dots.

When it is time to wrap up, call it:

"We have 15 minutes left. What progress have you made so far?"

"We have 10 minutes remaining. How would you like to wrap up today's session?"
A well-rounded wrap-up also includes:
- Outlining actions
- Defining timelines
- Exploring obstacles
- Inquiring about accountability or resources
- Confirming takeaways
- Inviting further learning

As you can see, an impactful wrap-up has a life of its own and goes well beyond just setting up actions.

TIPS ON TIMING & WRAP UP:

It is the coach's responsibility to keep the session on time, not the client's. Facilitating timing is about respect and boundaries.

CALLING TIME: To help a session wrap up, it is helpful to call the exact time. "We have 10 minutes left…." Calling the exact time invites the client to shift gears and wrap things up.

Avoid using evaluative language when calling the time. For example, stating "We are out of time" can place unintended pressure on the client.

RUNNING OVER: If you feel the session could run over, check-in with yourself, "Do I have time to run late?" Assuming it is acceptable for the client to run late can cause problems for the client. If you are chronically late starting sessions, this can cause frustration to the client.

- If you have time, check with your client: "I am noticing we may run late. I have time to give an extra 10 minutes. Would this help?" It is imperative to ask permission.
- If no, then state, "I have another client scheduled in a couple of minutes. What can we do to support you as we wrap up?" Call it. If a client had to wrap up and there were tears or a greater sense of being incomplete over something very stressful or urgent, it is best practice to give them a call later to check in on them.

NO SHIFT: In some sessions, the client will not have a shift. These are opportunities to invite homework for continued exploration. In these moments, call the time and begin the formal wrap-up. In the wrap-up, sometimes shifts can happen, and homework assignments can facilitate solutions.

Examples:

"We have 15 minutes left. What progress do you see you've made so far?"
"What do you see as some potential next steps?"
"What homework around are you willing to take on?"

CONSIDER:

What are the boundaries you want to have on your time? Do you want to charge for that time if a session runs over, or is that donated time?

Be clear and upfront in your contract. If I were a client and the coach ran late without asking permission and then billed me later, I would feel unsettled and begin to watch the clock.

Out of respect for the client, be very clear and upfront. You can also manage expectations in the initial longer Foundation Session. Let the client know your policy around session length. Some coaches are OK with always running over. Other coaches always wrap up sessions on time.

Helping the client know what to expect from you gives them a great sense of relief. Being a non-judgmental neutral observer also gives your clients the space to explore and grow.

BEING A BLANK SLATE

What does the term blank slate mean to you?

To me, it is like a chalkboard waiting to be written upon. Or a life waiting to be created.

Mary Morrisey, a motivational speaker and coach, invites people to consider your life as a book. On the left side, the past has been written. On the right side are blank pages waiting for you to fill in the rest.

What if life isn't just about finding yourself. What if life was also about creating yourself? This is coaching. Filling in the future, deciding what to write in the blank space of the chalkboard. One might assume babies come into the world as blank slates. We have found that this is not so. Babies are born with genetics, predispositions, and a body that has instincts. If you are a parent who has more than one child, I am confident you have observed just how different each child's predisposition is even though they came from the same parent.

At some point in our youth we all eventually have our first negative experience, our first wounding. We then receive messages from society, our parents, our friends, and the media.

- *"You are better than that."*
- *"You are clumsy."*
- *"You are not going to amount to anything if you do that."*
- *"You need to lighten up."*
- *"Why aren't you more like so and so?"*
- *"If you aren't a size eight you are overweight."*
- *"Please stop talking so much." "You need to get over being shy."*

As adults, we take our predisposition, add layers of these messages, conscious or unconsciously, and take them with us. Then neuropathways are formed as we gain experiences, good and bad.

- *Parents fighting*
- *Being bullied*
- *Being made fun of at school*
- *Being a straight-A student*
- *Being the failure*
- *Being the rock for others*

To masterfully coach another, we must learn to show up as a blank slate. What does that mean? Must we forget our own badges of wisdom when we coach?

We don't need to forget everything to be the blank slate. We must, however, put aside our biases, not our experiences. We must show up with a clean heart, ready to see what the client pulls out of the blank space of possibility. We must be open and spacious so that the client can work their magic.

Our experiences have shaped who we are. There is wisdom at the heart of our experiences. We do not have to leave our experiences at the door. We do need to learn how to use our experiences in service of the client. In other words, we do not want our experiences to bias and hijack the client. We want our contribution to the coaching process to be in service of the client.

Years ago, I was walking to my office. On the way there I always walked past the large, beautiful, fragrant orange trees on the outside terrace. I had been watching a cocoon to see when it might hatch. One day, it was shaking. I walked over and saw that the butterfly was in the process of ushering itself out of the cocoon. Wow!

One of my colleagues walked by. I was so excited that I waved for her to come and experience this with me. She came over and was just as thrilled as I was! One of our instructors walked by, and we both waved her over. She walked over. Wide-eyed, looking intently, she said, "Oh, my. I think it needs help. I think it is struggling!" She poked at it in an attempt to help it out. The entire chrysalis fell off the tree it was attached to and hit the ground. The butterfly trying to make its way did not make it.

I looked it up and learned that in order to live, the butterfly has to hang upside down for a certain amount of time to get enough blood to its wings so that it can fully expand and dry out.

Transformation is a process that is all about respecting timing and is based on spaciousness to expand undisrupted.

In coaching, you will sometimes be able to see things before your clients see them. You may see their wings fully expanded and envision them flying while they are still hanging upside down, wings crumpled and not sure what you are alluding to.

You might have an intuition that a choice may not be ultimately the best. While the client may need to experience this choice before they are fully ready to let go.

Trust your client. Trust the crumpled wings serve a process. Trust something within your client knows what to do. They have an internal compass.

CASE STUDY: A client of mine came to her session proud that she was embarking on a new career path. She quit a strenuous corporate career and decided to follow her heart. When she delivered the news, I was astonished and confused. The new career move didn't seem to reflect her values or come to what she shared she felt called to do. I also wondered about a discrepancy between her gifts and this new career. As a coach, I inquired about how she felt about the new career aligning with her bigger calling, gifts, and values. She said it did. I took a deep breath, and I honored her truth. We proceeded. Now, I have to be honest. My intuition was telling me this was not a good fit for her full potential. After I checked my intuition out, as a professional coach, it is my duty to show up neutral and in supportive alliance with the client's definition of their truth. So, I trusted the process, despite my gut instinct.

After months passed her new boss was asking her to sign falsified paperwork. This rubbed her integrity the wrong way and she came to the next session and said, "I'm out. This is not the right career move for me."

Her true shift occurred months later and after thousands of dollars were lost in training. Or so I thought.

Had my neutrality failed her? Could I have kept her from that negative experience? From losing all of that money and what seemed like a derailment from her true potential? We debriefed the experience. I shared my initial intuition and my commitment to honor her.

She thanked me for respecting her. She confided that she needed one "last hurrah!" before she stepped foot into her true calling. She shared that if she didn't have that final experience, that it would have haunted her for years, and now that she had the last hurrah out of her system, she could fully commit to her true calling, full steam ahead.

This client is now a wildly successful full-time business, executive, and life coach on our team. Her name is Tabitha, and the world is so fortunate she is now helping empower thousands of lives with her work as a coach.

This experience is an example of the trust we can grapple with as we are coaching. Can we see the butterfly crumpled up, hanging upside down, vibrating, and trust the transformational process?

Masterful coaches are responsive to the question: Is the client hanging upside down out of fear and not leaving the safety of the cocoon when they could be needing a challenge? Or, is the client enduring the transformational process and how can I hold space as they do so?

The mastery is in learning to trust the blank space where new potential will be born. Key points:
1. *If we take the client's words and interpretations at face value, we can join them in the problem.*
2. *We never know what may be the consequences of good fortune. We never know what might be the consequences of bad fortune.*
3. *Maybe life is spring boarding us to something better when it least seems that way.*

Clients have their own timing. Trust them. Even when it doesn't make logical or intuitive sense, trust them.

To help you along your journey of becoming a masterful coach, I wish to gift you with this parable:

Once upon a time, there was a Chinese farmer. One day his horse ran away. His neighbors, who gathered with him each evening, shared their pity and said, "That's truly unfortunate."

To their sentiment, he replied, "Maybe."

The next day his horse returned with seven wild horses with it. His neighbors that evening shared their enthusiasm and said, "Wow. That's truly fortunate!"

To their sentiment, he replied, "Maybe."

His son was taming one of the wild horses the next day, was thrown and broke his leg. His neighbors that evening shared their pity and said, "That's truly unfortunate."

To their sentiment, he replied, "Maybe."

The next day the military came to draft his son into the war. His son was rejected because of his broken leg. His neighbors that evening shared their enthusiasm and said, "Wow. That's truly fortunate!"

To their sentiment, he replied, "Maybe."

The word "maybe" is a gift along your coaching path. It will help you show up and honor the blank space the client will be filling in. "Maybe" is every masterful coach's best friend. It is a reminder to show up with a humble heart and trust. Maybe your intuition is helpful?

Maybe your "intuition" is your own concern? Maybe when your client laughs they are happy? Or, maybe laughter is their defense mechanism? Check with your client and honor their answer and process.

Masterful coaches do not assume and remember... maybe.

HOW TO AVOID HIJACKING

If I said that the coach "hijacked" the session, what comes to mind for you? Hijacking happens when the coach takes over the direction of a session by pushing their own opinion or agenda on a client. In therapy and consulting, the professional is hired to offer advice, take the lead, and make professional judgment calls.

- In coaching, we follow the client's lead.
- In coaching, to take over is to take the client's power from them.
- In coaching, we provide space, skills, and a process for the client to go deeper into the new realm of their unexplored potentials.

It is one thing to challenge a client or bring up concerns; it is another thing to take over and steer the client in a direction you want them to head.

Coaching is about 100% client agency, honoring that agency, and inviting that agency. Guess what?

We can be experts on external factors, processes, systems, etcetera. We are never the expert of another human being.

I don't typically speak in absolutes, but this is an absolute and bears repeating. *We are never the expert of another human being.*

This is good news and bad news. This is bad news because you will feel lost in sessions sometimes and you may not always know what to say or do next. This is good news because you get to take yourself off the hook, the client is 100% responsible for their results, and you will help them reach those results!

Remember the axiom:

> *Give someone a fish, and they are fed for a day.*
> *Teach someone to fish, and they are fed for a lifetime.*

Masterful coaching teaches us how to dig within ourselves for answers so that we tap into our own potential in all human domains.

Whose agenda is it?

No Agenda = The coach shows up without an agenda for the client.

On the one hand, we have no agenda for our client. In-session, the topic, direction, and outcomes are all established by the client.

Yet, the paradox is that we do have an agenda at that same time! We have one overarching agenda.

One Agenda = The coach still has the agenda for the client's success.

If our desire for their success turns into us pushing them in a particular direction, then we have hijacked the client's self-agency.

Hijacked Agenda = Coach has personal agenda or opinion of the client.

There are many paths to the top of the same mountain. Which path should you take? The one the client chooses. This is called "co-creating" the session.

All masterful sessions are co-created, and the coach even turns the session direction over to the client a few times to avoid any hijacking. Examples:
- What's next?
- Where to now?
- What question do you have for yourself now?
- What direction would you like to take next?

Some hijacking is conscious. Some hijacking is unconscious. The goal is to gain self- awareness so we can catch ourselves in the act of over-stepping the client and give the power back to the client.

Below are a few of the most common symptoms of hijacking so that you can begin to gain enough self-awareness to deeply honor your client by following their lead.

SYMPTOMS

1. **You feel** an *emotional attachment to the outcome.*
2. **You feel** *driven to "get it right."*
3. **You are** *working too hard and pushing them into an answer.*
4. **You are** *over-talking or oversharing or cheerleading them on.*

If you tell me you absolutely know a client's truth, what are you forgetting?

"Maybe"

BUILDING A BOAT

Here is the catch though!

We often can see something before a client can. We must remember the importance of timing, client readiness, and client perspective.

Use your insights to reflect back to the client what you see and question if your impressions or ideas land or hold value to them. If they don't land, that is great too. This is a cue to switch directions.

Keep in mind, if you provide an answer the client agrees with, there is less ownership over the idea than if the client generated the idea.

- ○ *Ownership comes when answers are self-generated.*
- ○ *If we "give them the fish" for the session, they didn't learn to fish.*
- ○ *Ownership is also a key ingredient to empowerment.*

Resist the urge to take away the client's opportunities to self-learn and self-generate.

Yes, there will be times to offer to help a client brainstorm. It is helpful to step in and offer help after you have invited the client to answer first. Then practice keeping your offers to a minimum to give the client space to generate.

In coaching, we go beyond teaching the client to fish. We also can help the client build a boat and travel even further than their initial goals.

5 COMMON HIJACKS

When I'm mentoring and listening to recorded sessions, if I notice a coach circles back more than twice to push a direction, this indicates to me that a potential hijack may be on the way.

It is one thing if a question doesn't land, and we switch gears to ask it another way. It is another thing to push a client towards an answer you want to hear.

It is one thing to challenge a client. It is another thing to keep challenging them to take the actions you want them to.

It is one thing to share a concern. It is another thing to share a concern and then press your point to sway them.

These are the five most common hijacks:
- o Intuitions
- o Personal projections
- o Fears / Concerns
- o Misperception
- o Cheerleading

INTUITIONS

How do you tell the difference between a projection and an intuition?

In coaching, we do not want to leave our intuition at the door. Intuition is a powerful human asset when used masterfully. Intuition can lead to powerful shortcuts and plant seeds for future growth.

The question is: How do we use our intuition in coaching *without* hijacking the client's agency?

Here are four things to consider:

1. Do not confuse your intuition as a reality for the client. Even if your intuition is correct, if the client is not ready, pushing the point can cause harm to the relationship.

2. Call it out and inquire: "I may be having an intuitive hit. Would you like to hear it?"

3. Deliver it as a question: "I am wondering if…." Stay inquisitive versus stating an intuition as a fact, like saying, "you are not ready."

4. Embody a take it or leave it attitude; it might feel significant to you, but it might not feel that big to the client. It is not personal.

Remember:

- Offering intuition can add to the client's process by providing a piece of the puzzle perhaps they couldn't have arrived at on their own. You honor them by letting them self-determine if the intuition is helpful or not.

- If an intuition doesn't land now, that is OK. Your contribution may have planted a seed for later when the timing might be ripe.

- The intuition may have been a personal projection. In coaching, we check "intuitions" out for validity and never assume we are right.

PERSONAL PROJECTIONS

Just because I am not a keynote speaker does not mean my client won't be a wildly successful one. Just because I have a stuck point doesn't mean my client has to have it too. If we have had a negative experience, a strong opinion, or a concern for the client, then our personal projections can interfere with the neutrality required for masterful coaching. The irony is that our past experiences and concerns for the client can also be of service to them.

The goal is not to leave parts of ourselves at the door but to offer our past experiences, questions, and thoughts completely unattached.

If you notice a projection or a personal trigger, these are steps you can take:
1. Notice the tug.
2. Set it aside for now.
3. Revisit outside of the session.
4. Seek additional support if needed.

MASTERY TIP: Never coach in an active wound. While it can be helpful to coach in areas you have overcome hardship, an active wound can lead us to carry a strong bias or to become emotionally triggered in a session.

If you find a bias or trigger coming up for you in sessions, you may want to seek the help of a coaching supervisor, mentor coach, or a therapist to work through what is coming up.

FEARS / CONCERNS

Your body has fears for a reason. To help keep you safe.

It is no different in coaching. Our fears and concerns can help contribute to the client's process.

The difference is how we handle them.

It is our responsibility and duty to share a fear or concern with a client. It is their responsibility to "take it or leave it."

CASE STUDY: My client shares with me, "I am quitting my job tomorrow! Woo-hoo!" This is news to me. They then share that they have no savings account or backup plan. It would be irresponsible of me not to run my concern by them. Yet, once I have done so, they are ultimately responsible for their choices. It is the role of a coach to sway them to my truth or idealism. It is our role as a coach to trust our clients through it all. Perhaps that "bad" choice we think they are making needs to happen for something more meaningful to unfold.

MISPERCEPTIONS

Have you ever been to a meeting where you missed what the presenter said but were too embarrassed to stop and ask them to go back? So you sit there confused, hoping they might repeat it? Leaving outcomes up to a "hope" is often not the most efficient strategy.

In coaching, if I pretend to have heard my client or pretend to understand where the client is heading, or trail off in thought, then I've left my client. If you ever feel confused in a session or missed something the client said, stop the session and get clear before proceeding. It is our duty to stay on track with the client, and if we veer off, to come back asap.

When confusion happens, we might accidentally ask questions or take a direction in complete opposition to what the client is offering. This is called accidental hijacking.

To avoid accidental hijacking:

> → Feel confused?
>> → Stop.
>>> → Interrupt.
>>>> → Get clear.
>>>>> → Proceed.

CHEERLEADING

Have you ever had someone praise you more than you felt you deserved, and it left you wondering what you missed?

In coaching, overpraising is called cheerleading.

Cheerleading happens when we push our positive ideas or energy onto the client to help them along. First of all, cheerleading has its place; however, if you wish to have deeper and richer sessions, there are considerations around cheerleading. When the coach gets excited before the client, we miss significant opportunities to go deeper.

For example, if I cheerlead by saying: "WOW, awesome work!! You are doing amazing. Look at you go!" they can feel more obligated to join me and:
- Wonder if they are missing something by not feeling the same way.
- Want the coach to approve of them, so they agree and ignore the deeper issue.
- Avoid the uncomfortable feelings, telling themselves they "should" feel happier like the coach does.

On the other hand, if I reflect the client's options and possibilities and then ask them how they felt hearing me reflect, I've opened the door for truth to walk through. Our neutrality gives the client time to reflect. They may respond with "I thought I'd be happier hearing those" or "I had a twinge of regret" or "I felt fear." In these instances, we get closer to the heart of the matter.

The beneficial side of cheerleading comes *after* the client gets excited.

The wisdom is in the placement. Example: "I heard you come up with [recap]. How do those feel to you?" If the client says "good!!" or "great!" then jump in with enthusiasm and celebrate with them. Example: "I am excited to see you step into these! Great job!"

CAVEAT: Notice if the client's words don't match the sentiment. If they say the recap felt "good," but their tone was flat versus excited, that is a cue to inquire about the discrepancy. Reflect and inquire. "You said "good," and yet your tone sounded lower. Is there anything there to explore further?"

We want to help identify any blockages to the client's success and help the client remove them or turn them into stepping stones.

Without the client generating the excitement, the outcome can also fall flat after the session ends. In other words, if the motivation comes from outside of themselves, then it is not embodied or owned in the same way. Extrinsic motivations, like will power, only last so long. Sometimes this is accidental. We can see a possibility for a client and get worked up before they do. If you catch yourself more excited or enthusiastic than the client, take a breath and return to the client to see where they are at.

In masterful sessions, we are present and intentional about honoring our clients. We set our own needs aside.

We also want to be conscious about how and when we share our thoughts and ideas. We want our shares to honor the client's truth and experience first.

Examples of sharing in ways that honor the client:

"When I hear about the opportunity you have to speak to the Chamber, I feel excited for you. What comes up for you though?"

"My hope for you is to feel so confident you shine. On a scale from one to ten, where are you at with embracing your confidence?"

"That sounds like an excellent opportunity. Congratulations, I am excited for you. How are you feeling about it though?"

When we share, it is best to own the share and immediately turn the session back over to the client. Leave an opening for them to have their own experience.

IN SUMMARY: If we cheerlead, a blockage may be overlooked and the client is left hanging. Sometimes cheerleading can be more intentional. Sometimes we want the client to feel excited. Be aware of your motivation to go faster than the client. Check-in with the client. Trust them, follow them, and when the excitement genuinely percolates up from within, celebrate with them!

EXAMPLES

In the example below, the client came to the session wanting to work on time management. The session is halfway through and they are exploring work dynamics. See if you can pick up on any bias from the coach.

Coach: OK, so you have identified you are working sixty hours a week. Is it time for a new job?

Client: Not at all! I love what I do. Yes, the hours are crazy, but I do not have any kids or a partner. It's just me. I really just need to manage my time better so I can fit in workouts and some occasional social time.

Coach: What about when you do get a partner. If you maintain this schedule will you have time for both?

Client: I hadn't thought about that. I think I can cross that bridge when/if it happens. I'm content right now. Work is very fulfilling.

Coach: I can imagine there has to be a part of you that feels sixty hours is just too much?

Client: No, not really. I really just need to be able to balance the time better, that is all. I do want to workout more, like I said.

Consider, what is your intention for pushing a client? Did you burn out from working 60 hours a week once?

It can help to remember that every person has their own success formula in life. Their success may look vastly different from yours.

DIRECT COMMUNICATION

A better way to go about having a strong opinion is through direct communication.

Coach: OK, so you have identified you are working sixty hours a week. Is it time for a new job?

Client: Not at all! I love what I do. Yes, the hours are crazy, but I do not have any kids or a partner. It's just me, so I'm ok with the sixty hours. I really just need to manage my time better so I can fit in workouts and some occasional social time.

Coach: Can I be honest for a moment. Client: Yes, please do.

Coach: When I hear sixty hours, I feel worried about burnout or your future life-balance. Just double-checking: Is there anything to this that worries you?

Client: Well, I see what you are saying and have actually thought about that too. I came to realize...no, not really. I really just need to be able to balance my time better currently and have it include more of a workout schedule. I thoroughly love what I do and derive a lot of fulfillment from it!

Coach: Got it! I completely understand and want to acknowledge you for knowing where your alignment is right now in your life. Where are we headed next?

As you can see, the coach still offered concern and then honored the client's truth. Direct communication is honest and does not include directing the direction.

> *"We are here*
> *to be of service to our client's there."*
> ~ Nancy Smyth

Notice in your coaching. If you are not letting something go, pause and return to the client's agenda.

What about sharing a personal story? Is sharing hijacking?

SHARING PERSONAL STORIES

Sharing can be a way to connect. Oversharing can lead to a disconnect.

The first thing to consider is, what is the intention for sharing?
1. Is my share concise?
2. Does my sharing serve the client?
3. Does my story offer empathy or help illustrate a concept?
4. Am I sharing to get my own needs met?

Next time you feel the urge to share, remember to WAIT = Why Am I Talking?

If you decide to share, keep it short and then turn it back on the client to see if it helped.
- "Does my experience reflect anything you are going through?"
- "What do you think about the experience I just shared?"
- "Does anything about what I shared help?"
- "Does that help?"

CLIENT REQUESTS FOR ADVICE

Have you heard your client tell you, "I would like your advice around this." Or ask you, "What do you think?"

Even after a client understands that coaches do not give advice, it is common for requests for advice to come up still. Requests for advice are a slippery slope. If we concede, we allow the client to defer their self-agency.

There are a few reasons a client may ask for advice. These reasons can be helpful to keep in mind.

1. They don't want to take full ownership or responsibility for the answer if it is high risk.

2. They are giving their power away by looking up to others to have their answers.
3. They don't yet fully believe in themselves.
4. They haven't experienced that they can trust themselves.
5. They feel stuck and want help generating ideas or new thoughts.

There are a few helpful ways to navigate these requests while honoring the client and not hijacking their agency.

One surprisingly effective approach is to ask them for their ideas first.

> *Client: "What do you think I should do?"*
> *Coach: "What do you think you should do?"*

I say surprisingly because the client is often surprised they did have an answer after all. Sometimes this approach generates an answer or, they may say:

> *Client: "I'm not sure; that is why I want to know your opinion."*
> *Coach: "Fair enough. If you did know the answer, what would it be?"*

Nine times out of ten, the client has an answer they are just hesitant to share. Other times an answer is just beneath the surface. When the coach does not allow the client to defer, this invites the client to dig deeper within themselves. The client learns to fish.

Remember: Give someone a fish, they are only fed for a day. Giving a fish is a Band-Aid and doesn't get to the root of why the client is feeling stuck.

What about this scenario:

> *Coach: "How can I support you today?"*
> *Client: "I would love your advice on how I should approach my issue."*

What if the client's agenda is for the coach to give advice?

Remember, even if we have expertise, or do advise, how our expertise relates to the client is still in their hands and their inner truth is beyond the coaching scope. Getting them to their truth is within our scope and is our coaching duty.

> Coach: "I hear you want my advice. Just a reminder, I believe you carry your wisest answers for you, and I believe you are the expert in your life. What ideas have you thought of so far to approach this issue?"

The coach put the onus back to the client and reminded them that we believe the client is their own best expert and has what they need to succeed.

If the client still pushes for ideas, we can contribute and still honor their process. For example:

> Coach: "I have seen people have success applying X, Y, Z. What do you think about any of those?"

There may be a point where contributing to the client's thought process may help. If we contribute, immediately turn the conversation back to the client to see if anything offered was helpful. Take it or leave it.

> Coach: "In my experience with management, I saw A, B, C help. Do any of those ideas pertain to your situation?"

I recall asking one of my coaches for her advice. She responded by challenging me. "Laurel, why give your power away? I do not have your answers. But, I trust that *you* do." And then she smiled and allowed me to squirm in my discomfort of wanting someone to just tell me what to do!

At first, I felt frustrated that she said no. I wanted someone to just to guide the way, tell me what to do, and give me the solution.

I was later so grateful she set that boundary. I learned a lot about myself and grew into a new level of authority and fortitude in my life because she refused to allow me to give my power to her.

SUMMARY:

1. First, put the question back on the client. "I'd love to hear what you think first."
2. Second, challenge them. "If you did have the answer, what would it be?"
3. Third, invite them to contribute more. "What other ideas do you have?"
4. Last, if they remain stuck, contribute your idea and immediately hand the direction back to the client. "Was any of that useful to your situation?"

What do we do when a need for advice or support goes beyond the professional scope of coaching? We will explore this next.

WHEN & HOW TO REFER OUT

In coaching, we are trained to understand our scope of practice thoroughly. We draw a clear line between coaching and therapy. If a client cannot "hold the coaching," make progress, increase self-awareness, take ownership and action, then a professional coach will refer out.

Therapists are educated and licensed to diagnose and treat traumas, give direction and help someone gain agency or heal emotional wounds.

Sometimes when a client is unable to hold the coaching, there may be something unresolved going on.

As a coach, we can reflect back the lack of progress we observe and see if the client feels they need a deeper level of support.

Some coaching clients may need both. Some clients may be in therapy to work on healing and work with their coach on self-development and goals.

If a client is missing information, we can refer them to a consultant and continue to coach the client. In coaching, we also help clients locate resources, accountability, and missing ingredients to their success.

REFERRING OUT - Example A:

Client's agenda: "My dad is maddening, toxic, and emotionally abusive and I need a self- care strategy for when I have to be around him."

The coach can say: "I am sorry to hear. Just to be clear, this area is outside of my scope of practice. While I can coach you to find a self-care strategy for being around your family, I will not be able to guide you in family dynamics that you may need to consider as you are navigating this issue. Do you want to proceed or seek the guidance of a family therapist at this point?"

If the client decides to proceed, the boundary has been established, and the coach would help the client self-determine self-care. The coach may still suggest the client consults with a therapist in addition to the coaching.

The above scenario is of an established client that wanted support in a single session around the family dynamic. The client's overall coaching purpose is to be a more intentional wife and partner. That was an example of handling a one-off agenda issue; however, if a potential client comes to the coach and wants coaching to address the problems around their "toxic and abusive" family members, that would be a referral out to a licensed therapist. Taking on a client that could benefit more from a therapist than a coach would be unethical and a high-liability risk for the coach.

REFERRING OUT - Example B:

A woman is looking to hire a health coach. Her goal is to work through emotional eating. The coach asks: "Option to pass on answering this question: Does any of your emotional eating stem from past abuse or trauma?"

This potential client chose to answer and says "yes." The coach informs the client that this is outside of the scope of coaching and that coaching may or may not work.

The coach asks if she has done any therapy around the past traumas. She says yes and feels she is ready for coaching. The coach offers to start with one month of coaching to see if the coaching will work and be the best option for the client.

They agree to move forward under this agreement.

The coaching worked very well in this case study, and the client had done enough therapy to "hold the coaching." If that wasn't the case and after one month of support the client couldn't hold the coaching, the coach would be responsible for referring out.

What it may look like if this client was not able or willing to "hold the coaching" and hadn't done therapy yet on past traumas:

- Ongoingly comes to sessions without making any progress and can't figure out why.
- The problems brought up feel emotionally overwhelming and unsafe.
- The client shows up not able to self-reflect.

What if the potential client chose to pass on answering the question? In this scenario, the coach can approach it like this:

Coach: "Option to pass on answering this question: Does any of your emotional eating stem from past abuse or trauma?"

Potential client: "I'll pass."

Coach responds: "No problem at all; I respect your choice. I do need to share that in the event a past trauma may be an issue, it is outside of the scope of practice of coaching to address. In these circumstances, I cannot guarantee coaching will be effective. In coaching, we focus on goals and strategy and self-growth. If you would like to try coaching out for a session and see if it resonates, we can do that. If you ever feel like you need a deeper level of support, I have resources to refer to."

You will need to establish your professional boundaries and scope as a coach. If there is any area you are not comfortable coaching around, you do not have to take on that client and can refer out, even if it is to another coach.

Questions to consider:
1. *What situations would I be uncomfortable coaching around?*
2. *What is my referring out process?*
3. *Who will I refer to? (Create a list of other coaches and therapists.)*

THE THREE CONSIDERATIONS

There are three considerations when referring out. 1) Is the purpose for the coaching in the realm and scope of coaching? 2) If maybe, can the client hold the coaching and work with a therapist simultaneously? 3) If not, how can I help them find a licensed therapist or another professional?

My original niche was health coaching. I had written a book on the process of breaking free from emotional eating. I made it a point to ask potential clients if the emotional eating was linked to past trauma. When coaching on that topic, I find the cause can be either trauma induced or a stress response. I make it a point to ask upfront to gauge if I'm operating within my scope.

As coaches, we want to be honest and clear about scope.

When I'm meeting with a prospect, I have three buckets to help me determine the scope.
1. Yes, I firmly believe I can help you. From what you defined as your purpose for coming into coaching, I see coaching as an excellent fit for attaining those goals. Would you like to hear about my program options?
2. I am going to be completely honest. Based on what we discussed so far, I do not know if coaching will be effective. It depends on how you relate to

the process. Would you like to move forward on a trial basis, two to three sessions, and see how you feel? At a minimum, we will get you a strategy in place.

3. Unfortunately, this is outside of my scope of practice. I do not want you to waste any time or money. Let me get you some resources to put you in touch with someone who specializes in this area.

Being a successful coach requires integrity. It can be hard to turn away a client when we are just starting out and excited to get a new client; however, the risk is not worth it and places the client at an unfair advantage.

Coaching Scope	Situational Scope	Outside Of Scope
• Goals • Personal growth • Professional growth	• Bigger issues have already been worked on in therapy and client is ready to grow	• Abuse • Trauma • Addiction • Family dysfunction

The above are general guidelines. Depending on someone's background, they may be able to increase their coaching scope. For example, suppose a coach is a retired psychologist. In that case, they may coach around family or addiction more effectively than a coach with zero background or training in a topic.

The bottom line: Know your scope and be upfront. Learn your comfort levels and draw your professional boundaries to establish integrity in your practice.

Up next, let's dive into the coaching skills to begin to develop and gain awareness around.

CULTIVATING EXPLICIT & IMPLICIT SKILLS

Then there are implicit coaching skills that happen internally. There are observable coaching skills that are explicit. Below is a high-level overview of each. Masterful coaches engage the internal to inform the external.

Explicit skills are the skills we demonstrate in a session. They are observable and experienced by the client.

Newer coaches: Below is a list of the explicit coaching skills you will learn to hone in coach training. These are listed out so that you can begin to familiarize yourself with them as you start practice coaching.

Seasoned coaches: Below is a refresher from your coach training and hopefully some added perspectives to consider as you continue to grow as a coach.

CLARIFYING

In coaching, our job is to help our clients weed through how they feel, what they really need, what they genuinely desire and deeply value. We help them explore discrepancies in their beliefs, examine the inner meaning behind their words, settle on their intentions, and clarify their priorities.

Clarifying the agenda is the first goal in a session. The coaches I know who do not clarify the agenda and just dive in often miss the mark of what the client is really needing.

The next goal is to invite the client to greater overall clarity.

REFLECTION: Observations

I look at my client and they are scrunching their forehead as they talk about work. In an attempt to empathize, I say, "I can see you are upset."

What mark did I miss?

I interpreted what I saw without checking in with the client. I am assuming. I might be right, or I might have closed the door on something deeper or truer.

Masterful coaching is very clean. We stay in facts and do not stray into judgment or evaluation of the client. We remain neutral and open to any outcome the client has to offer. If I was neutral, I could have shared the facts of the observation and invited the client to share what was true for them. Example: "I noticed as you talk about work your forehead is scrunched. What's behind this for you?" Be completely open. The client may take a direction the coach couldn't have guessed.

Most missteps in coaching are paved with really good intentions. We mean well; we want our clients to move forward and succeed Sometimes our desire can lead us to take shortcuts or miss essential nuances.

If I interpret the client's reaction for them, I am leading. I am also potentially taking away their opportunity for fuller expression.

Practice reflecting only the facts of your observation. Some examples:
1. "When you shared, your voice elevated just then. What happened?"
2. "Did you notice as you talked about this option your face scrunched?"
3. "I heard your tone drop. What just came up?"

Now, let's look at the same examples above but have the coach interpret what is going on and leading the client:
1. "When you shared, I could hear how excited you were!" If the client didn't identify they were excited, then the coach is interpreting the elevated voice.
2. "Did you notice as you talked about this option you became uncomfortable?" The coach is interpreting the client's face scrunching.
3. "I hear the disappointment in your voice." The coach is assuming the tone drop is a disappointment.

These are great examples of what to avoid. Let the client self-determine. It helps them grow in their self-awareness, and it helps you learn about your client. Masterful coaches state the observation and drop the interpretation.

REFLECTION: Verbatim

When I first started coaching, I didn't realize that I interpreted just about everything my clients shared. It was an unconscious default I had. I learned to be aware of this: It is powerful when the client hears their own words reflected back to them. We often speak and don't fully hear our own words. Reflecting back verbatim words honors the client's truth and helps locate discrepancies. As I reflect my client's words, not mine, I hear, "Yes. That is it!" and they feel validated or solid. Or, I may hear, "I said that? Wow. I didn't realize it." Hearing our exact words furthers our self-knowledge and ability to note if we are on track or off. We honor the client when we use their words, not ours. Practice reflecting verbatim, single words or phrases that the client uses. Gift them the opportunity to hear themselves.

MASTERY TIP #1: As always in coaching, as my mentor Sandy put it, "different times, different things." There is a time and place for reworking the client's words. If we are inviting the client to a new perspective, we may offer a reword.

MASTERY TIP #2: If you can't recall the exact words your client used, you can offer your interpretation and call it out. Example: "I recall you saying something about wanting to face your fears. My interpretation. Is that close to what you meant?" Or, you can ask the client to recap. Example: "Can you recap for me the top three fears you identified so far?"

REFLECTION: Summarizing

I've heard two approaches to summarizing: bullet-pointing and paragraphs. I'm going to cut to the chase on this one. If you are not yet good at bullet-pointing back, practice this. When the coach dives into paragraphs of what the client said when reflecting back, it takes time away from the client. Instead, bullet point back key concepts by condensing them into one or two words. Below are examples of concise reflections. Example A is a paragraph format. Example B is an example of an effective bullet point.

Example A: So, I am hearing that you are really excited about the idea of a promotion, and it may take a few months; however, while you are waiting, you are looking at other companies and you want to find someone to redo your resume. You aren't sure if you found someone good or not. Also, you are waiting on references for them so you can see if you would be wasting your money or if it is worth the investment.

Example B: "OK. I've heard:
- Potential promotion
- Timing and
- Effective resume. Anything else?"

In masterful coaching, the coach concisely captures the client's keywords or phrasing, helps the client laser in, and moves the session forward efficiently.

INVITATIONS

Coaching is future-focused. While we might go into the past for information, we don't stay there. We invite our clients to establish what they want. We invite them into new perspectives or new ways of thinking.

Inviting is not the same as leading. We are not inviting them to see our side. We are inviting them to expand and access their wisdom.

Some examples of invitations:
- *What is the positive side to this?*
- *What if I said there were three opportunities in this challenge?*
- *Are you open to looking at this through a new lens?*
- *What is a new lens you could look through?*
- *What else needs to be considered?*
- *What does the solution look like? Feel like?*
- *How willing are you to shift?*
- *How might you approach this with an open heart?*
- *How could this be different?*

Notice how open and inviting these questions are. Practice inviting the new perspective to come from the client. Invitations are at the heart of masterful coaching!

EMPATHY

"Oh, wow. That sucks." Or?

"I am so sorry. I can only imagine how hurt you feel."

In the first example, I'm evaluating, judging, or agreeing with a story someone shared with me. We call this sympathy. You are sympathizing with the story or situation when you agree with it. "Yes, that is bad." "Oh, wow, how horrible."

Empathy is not about the story or the evaluation of the story. It is about reflecting back the feelings and needs of the person experiencing the story they are in.

Guess what?

We don't get out of the story by staying in the story. In coaching, we steer away from sympathy and deliver supportive empathy. Empathy gets to the heart of the matter.

"I know how much you value community; I can imagine you feel alone right now." "I am so sorry and can imagine how sad you feel." "I can imagine you need more connection right now."

When we are heard at a heart level, we feel safer, and we can exhale. Empathy is a powerful tool in coaching. It allows us to go deeper and use emotions as a reflection tool without crossing over into therapy.

It is a complete myth that emotions only belong in therapy. We are emotional beings. Emotions are a normal part of our work life, home life, social life, etcetera.

Emotions are powerful and direct
indicators of what we believe and perceive.

Emotions show us where we are in alignment with our values and out of alignment. To include them in the coaching equation is impactful and highly effective when approached correctly. Including emotional intelligence in sessions is incredibly impactful to the clients that do not consider themselves "touchy-feely" types. Broadening their emotional language opens up an entirely new world and expands this powerful domain of intelligence.

Dr. Marshal Rosenburg outlines an insightful four-step process for delivering empathy in the book Nonviolent Communication. He suggests that we include these ingredients when offering empathy:
1. State what is factual about what happened. Release evaluations and judgments.
2. Identify what emotions are present.
3. Identify the person's needs or values being impacted by what happened.
4. Ask how you can be supportive.

This process is called Compassionate Communication. It is a potent approach to delivering empathy and also an excellent tool for coaching around communication.

FORMING QUESTIONS

Questions are keys. Questions unlock new ideas and doorways. Questions engage the whole brain and get a client to dig deeper or think broader. There are a variety of questions coaches use to engage their clients in new ways. Each type of question serves a purpose.

We also look at the placement of a question. Closed or leading questions get a bad rap. Yet, there are times when they help the coaching process. Again, "different times, different things."

Below is a taxonomy of questions to become familiar with. Notice when a type of question is helpful and when it could be limiting.

Closed Questions: Eliciting a one-word answer, or yes/no.

> **Helpful:** 1) Client gets stuck in oversharing. 2) Coach needs to clarify.
> **Un-helpful:** Client is withdrawn and introverted, prone to under-sharing.
> **Examples:** "Do you like filing papers?" or "Do you want help?"

Open Questions: Invites creative open-ended thought.

> **Helpful:** 1) Client needs to explore or dig deeper. 2) In the body of the session.
> **Un-helpful:** 1) Client is overwhelmed. 2) Wrapping up a session on time.
> **Examples:** "What do you think about that?" "What else?" "Other ideas?"

Leading Questions: Invites a directed answer.

> **Helpful:** 1) Keeping a client on track. 2) Wrapping up a session on time.
> **Un-helpful:** Mid-session, when a client needs to explore or think broader.
> **Examples:** "What was good about school today? Vs. "How was school today?"

Process Questions: Inviting deeper thinking or analysis.

Helpful: 1) Client needs to consider multiple angles. 2) Homework assignments.
Un-helpful: Wrapping up a session on time. Action steps are needed.
Examples: "Reflecting on X, Y and Z, what values are your emotions linked to?"

Assumptive: Assuming the client has an answer or knowledge.

> **Helpful:** Inviting the client to see positive or significant aspects to something.
> **Un-helpful:** If it is leading the client and they need open processing.
> **Example:** "What do you like about dinner with your mother?"

Funneling: Sequentially corralling the client to a specific answer. Starts open, then moves to closed and leading.

> **Helpful:** Creating specific action steps. Exploring obstacles to actions.
> **Unhelpful:** In coaching = hijacking the agenda.
> **Example:** "When are you going to the store? What won't you get at the store? Isn't chocolate on your unhealthy list too?"

Rapport and Empathy: Connects with the client emotionally.

> **Helpful:** Honoring emotionally impactful moments. Help client feel heard.
> **Un-helpful:** Over-focusing on the emotional state of a problem.
> **Example:** "I recall your mother is in the hospital. How are you doing today?"

Clarifying: Compare and contrast, or stopping the session to clear up confusion.

> **Helpful:** 1) Agenda-setting. 2) If there is a discrepancy. 3) Coach is confused.
> **Un-helpful:** Asking client to over-clarify every word or statement.
> **Example:** "In the past you mentioned you are good at emotional intimacy but not physical. What is the difference to you?"

CONSIDERATIONS:
- *What is needed to help support the client?*
- *What are my motivations for asking?*
- *Are my questions reflecting my own bias?*
- *How many open questions can I ask in the body of the session?*
- *Is this good timing?*

MAKING OFFERS

Yes, we show up as a blank slate for our client. Yet, we do not leave our experiences at the door or on a shelf when we start to coach. We are a whole person, coaching another whole person.

Our background and experiences can perhaps benefit the client. Instead of leaving yourself out of the equation, consider making offers.

An offer is a thought, idea, or personal experience that may lend to the client's thinking. How we deliver an offer makes all the difference. We don't want to derail the client. We want to be of service.

Examples:

> "May I offer a different thought on that? – What if you were to...?" "Have you considered the idea of....?"
> "I have an idea. What about...?"

We want to use offers with care and caution. This section is not permission to push your opinion on the client. An offer is not a way to interject our opinion or guide the client to our solutions.

An offer should complement the client's exploration and broaden their thinking if they are getting stuck.

MASTERY TIP:

Pose an offer or contribution as a question. Or make a statement and ask the client what they think. For example, in my coaching practice, I use spiritual principles. My offers tend to look more like this: "May I offer a spiritual perspective? (Client gives permission.) There is a Sufi teaching that fear is half a message, reflecting what we don't want. Your heart has the other half of the message, reflecting what we do want. I'm curious what your heart is aching for here?"

– OR –

"A Course in Miracles teaches that fear is our responsibility. What do you think about that notion?"

Notice the coach makes an offer and then directly follows up to ask the client what they think. If we make offers as statements or quotes, or thoughts, we want to turn it back over to the client to see if it was of value or not. Take it or leave it. If an offer does not land, that is OK. It is good information about how we can learn from our clients and support them even better.

ENCOURAGEMENT & ACKNOWLEDGMENT

If I say "good job!" is that a fact, a form of encouragement, or a judgment call?

It may be all three. Let's go deeper.

Encouragement and acknowledgment are ways we support our clients. It is how we believe in our clients when they don't yet fully believe in themselves. It is how we celebrate our client's successes with them. In coaching, we want to be conscious and understand the distinctions between acknowledging, encouraging, and "cheerleading." We also want to understand the variety of ways we can deliver an acknowledgment without coming across as the expert evaluating them as if they are doing it "right." We are accustomed to speaking in evaluative language such as "Good work! Good job!" There is nothing wrong with this; however, if we over-rely on evaluative language, we miss the opportunity to deliver full support and even connect valuable integration points for our client.

> *Deeper acknowledgments*
> *Connect points of integration*
> *And invite depth of work.*

If I say "Good work!" how would you feel? Probably positive.

What if I said, "I can see how much your value for compassion is demonstrated in your new approach at work." Which one goes deeper? "Good work" feels good to hear, while an acknowledgment of who we are, what we value, reflects the essence of ourselves at a soul level and goes much, much, deeper.

Let's practice.

1. "Good work on that project!"

> Answer 1: The above statement is an evaluation.
>
> Answer 2: The above statement is a fact.

2. "I see how *deeply* you value contribution."

> Answer 1: The above statement is an evaluation.
>
> Answer 2: The above statement is a fact.
>
> Answer 3: The above statement contains both: evaluation and fact.

3. "I am happy to see you are leading this project through your value of integrity. How does that feel?"

> Answer 1: The above statement is an evaluation.
>
> Answer 2: The above statement is factual.

ANSWER KEY:

The first statement is answer number one. *"Good" is evaluative.*

The second statement is answer number three. "Deeply" the coach is judging and evaluating the depth. The exception is if the client self-identifies "I deeply value contribution," and the coach reflects the client's language to them. If this were the case, then the answer would be number two.

The last statement is answer number two. "I am happy" reflects how the coach feels, and the coach is expressing that feeling. The second part of the statement, "you are leading through your value of integrity" is the coach reflecting the client's truth back to the client and acknowledging the client.

Tips:

- Don't worry about feel-good evaluations here and there. They do feel good to receive! They have their place and are concise.
- At least two to three times in a session, gift the client with a deeper acknowledgment.

Here are some ways to practice:
- I want to recognize you for..
- I want to acknowledge how..
- I appreciate…
- I noticed how…
- I feel…when I see how…
- I see…
- I understand…

Coaching Mastery Practice:

Take a moment and identify a person at work, home, and a friend. Write down how you wish to share a deeper acknowledgment with them.

Example: My mom. "I want to share how much I appreciate your care and support of our family during a time that is not easy."

WHOLE-PERSON INQUIRY

"How many areas of your life are being impacted?" "What are you learning about yourself?"

"How can you apply your learning today to other areas of your life?" "Who do you need to be to make this happen?"

These questions invite client integration.

These questions combine the client's why with the who and the what so that they can effectively master how. These questions connect to bigger picture implications.

In essence, whole-person inquiry invites our client to connect life's dots. Whole-person coaching is well-rounded by including values, beliefs, emotions, thoughts, perspectives, perceptions, and somatic responses.

After you have been coaching for a while, notice if you default to any patterned way of inquiry. For example, if you default to "How do you feel about that?", you can round out your approach with, "What are you believing?" or "What sensations do you feel in your body?"

Masterful coaches also engage the client's wholeness. When clients begin to live, lead, and love their lives through their wholeness, they experience life in new ways. They may feel fulfillment, inner peace, and empowerment for the first time.

One powerful way is to remind them of your belief in their wholeness. For example: "I don't have your answers. I have my answers and trust you have yours. I believe you are whole and complete and have everything you need."

Confirming our belief in our clients codifies a core principle of coaching. Each of us is whole, resourceful, and complete. We do have everything we need to succeed within us.

Implicit Coaching Skills

MINDSET

What makes the difference between a conversation between friends and a coaching conversation?

A lot.

When we speak to friends, we tend to have opinions, past experiences that we bring into our conversations. We naturally agree and sympathize with friends. These are great attributes for friendship. When I call a friend after a hard day, I love to hear, "Yes, that sounds horrible!"

If my coach said this, I would take a pause. I want my coach to see above my experience and not always agree with me. Masterful coaches hold space with an open, neutral, and positive mindset yet offers challenge.

Open mindset = What if there are three opportunities in this challenge?

Neutral mindset = "This is a safe space. There are no good-bad, right-wrong answers."

Positive mindset = What are three positive ways to view this challenge?

ENERGY

Our mindset lends to the energy we bring into the session. In masterful coaching, our energy is an open and spacious container for the client. What do you need to hold your energy in an open, positive, neutral, and spacious way? Being aware of our energy helps us sense what is going on in more profound ways with our clients. My MCC mentor coach invited me to explore my coaching energy as in front of me (focused), above me (open to wisdom), and behind me (intuitive). I realized I was coaching from my energy focused forwards and above. When I added the focus of my energy to be opened all around me, my ability to attune to my clients expanded in new, more intuitive ways.

Where is the focus of your energy as you coach?

Are you aware of your energy?

What do you do to prepare your energy for a session?

SENSING

Masterful coaches are also aware of the client's energy. I was in a session with master coach Nancy Smyth. It was a phone session. She asked me a question. This time the question didn't land for me. My energy dipped away. I was silent and didn't course-correct the conversation or let her know the question didn't land.

"Where did you go just now?" she asked.

This was an astonishing moment. How did she know I wasn't quietly processing the question? Normally when I'm quiet, I am processing a question, and she provides space for that. This time, she sensed I was not with her at this moment. She felt it.

This is a powerful example of sensing the client.

If you study quantum physics, you learn that the principles of time and space do not apply to energy. Everything is energy in different forms. There is a part of us that is intuitively attuned to the energy of our clients.

Coach from attunement.

PRESENCE & ESSENCE

Presence is about being in the present moment and not overly swayed by our thoughts. Being in the moment with a client is where we notice the tiniest cues a client is giving off. If we leave the present moment, we have left the client. If we are overthinking, we will miss the subtle cues.

Presence also carries an energy awareness. Presence is a state of being, not a state of mind. With presence, we can connect with our client's energy, intentionally using our own energy to invite shifts.

Being attuned to the energy and essence of our client is the heart of masterful coaching. Meeting a client in this way engages the core of the client's potential.

- ✓ How can I remain fully present with my client's energy?
- ✓ Can my energy align to support my client authentically?
- ✓ Can my presence invite new ways of being?
- ✓ Can I recognize when it is time to shift my energy in support of the client?

INTUITION

Intuition in coaching is interesting. How can you tell the difference between fear and intuition? Or how about the difference between intuition and personal projection?

I once had the opportunity to go to Germany. I was petrified of flying. When I was 15, I was in a horrific car accident where I was flung from a truck going 80 miles an hour on the freeway. I live with a substantial PTSD response when it comes to anything fast-moving, even rollercoasters. Before leaving for Germany, I felt this powerful "intuition" telling me the plane would crash. I almost canceled because the feeling was so strong. I decided to go anyway. I went and Germany was incredible! No plane crashes. I confused my intuition with intense fear.

Using intuition in coaching can be very powerful; however, we want to ensure that we are dealing with actual intuition and not assumptions or other emotions. Below are some considerations about intuition in general and how to effectively use intuition in coaching.

As I look back over my life, I asked my intuition how to tell a true intuition from a strong emotional reaction. The answer I received? True intuition carries matter-of-fact energy to them. Emotional reactions will always have a strong push or pull energy to them. It is easy to confuse emotional pulls as intuitions because emotional reactions feel so real. Mastery is understanding the differences.

As we grow in our coaching mastery, we learn to develop our intuition and our intuitive type.

There are four primary intuition types: (12)
   1. Visual: Seeing flashes or images in the mind. As your client is talking, do you get flashes of images beyond what they are sharing?

2. Emotional: Feeling empathically others' feelings. When you start a session, do you all of a sudden feel an emotion, like sadness? Then your client shares that today is very sad for them?
3. Cognizant: Inner-knowing. Do you receive answers when you ask a question? Almost as if someone else just provided it.
4. Audient: Hearing an inner voice. Do you experience your mind guiding you?

Most people embody one as a primary and may have another as a secondary. For example, my primary is cognizant, and my secondary is visual.

Here are some questions to help you hone your intuitive skills in your coaching:

o *How do I experience intuition?* Knowing your type can help you determine if you have an intuition or just a thought/projection/idea.

o *How can I best use intuition in sessions and still honor my client's process?* You can have a go-to saying like, "May I offer an idea? I'm wondering if I have an intuitive hit."

o *What environment or conditions supports my intuition?* I am a phone coach. My intuition is ten times stronger over the phone when the visual isn't distracting me. Learn what conditions heighten your intuition and you can structure your practice around it.

How about beyond specific skills? How can we begin to listen beyond words or address discrepancies? Up next, we look at both of these coaching capacities.

LISTENING FOR WHAT IS NOT SAID

I have a confession. Coaching never came naturally to me. My mentor coach said, "Laurel, you are working too hard. Let your client do the work." I had an unconscious assumption that "the harder I worked, the more value the client would take away." Have you felt this yet? Most coaches do, especially when starting out. The more I let go of the reins, the more coaching felt effortless. I found myself finishing a session and so grateful to get paid to do something that began to feel so effortless and yet was profoundly helpful to the client.

There were two aspects to coaching that completely stumped me:
1. How does one listen to what is not said?
2. How do masterful coaches form powerful questions?

I saw coaches who effortlessly, masterfully, elegantly accomplished both, and I would listen in awe. "Wow, how do they have those magic powers I was somehow born without?"

My quest began to compute what felt like was incomputable. I discovered that the two categories that stumped me the most were the same two categories that were interconnected and linked.

In essence:

Listening beneath the surface
helps produce more powerful questions.

When I say "powerful questions" what comes to mind for you?

What makes a question powerful?

Is a powerful question always challenging? Is a powerful question always profound?

Powerful questions help create openings, invite shifts, and evoke new awareness. Powerful questions go beyond what is said and are formed by listening and guessing what is not being said. More good news! Listening beneath the surface is also how we can help locate "the Big A," which is the larger agenda that the client is not fully aware of.

There are six high-impact coaching skills to help us get beneath the surface and listen for what is not said.

These are:

1. Somatic observations
2. Identifying the "yes" behind the no
3. Metaphor
4. Mindset pitfalls
5. Unspoken feelings, needs, values
6. Intuitions

1. Somatic observations:

Noticing a discrepancy between the client's words and their tone of voice takes them deeper. Example: "YES, I'm SO excited!!!" versus: "Ya, that is exciting." (flat tone) We will cover the full gambit of somatics in another segment.

2. Identify the "Yes" behind the "No":

Being aware of the yes behind the no is one of the most potent ways to hear what is not being said and often the most overlooked. If someone told you:

"I hate the political landscape. I hate all of the fighting, the ignorance, the intolerance. It leaves me disgusted."

What do you imagine I value? Equality, respect, and cohesion perhaps?

When we face a problem, it is easier to identify what we don't like or want. As coaches, we can use our client's "no" to reflect a potential "yes!" What is on the flip side? What does our client's heart really desire deep down? Take them there. See what is beneath the surface.

3. Metaphor:

Metaphor is a powerful way to engage deeper, beneath the surface thinking. Often, we speak in metaphor without realizing it. Reflecting back to the client the metaphors they use helps them raise awareness and invite depth.

4. False Beliefs:

False beliefs stem from fears. Helping a client identify the fear can help them get out of it. There is a Sufi teaching that fear is only half a message. It reflects to us what we don't want. Our heart has the other half of the message, reflecting back to us what we do want. We can use false beliefs as avenues to help our clients steer from fear to clear.

5. Unspoken Feelings, Needs, Values:

When our clients speak to an issue on a surface level, we can help them go deeper by assisting them to identify their unspoken feelings, needs, and values.

6. Intuition:

As we've explored, intuition can be a powerful shortcut. Offer your intuitive hits. "I may be getting an intuitive hit around this. Would you like to hear?" See what happens. The thing to remember about intuitive hits:

- You may be wrong or it may not land. That is OK. Transition back to the client's intuition.
- You may have planted a seed that will sprout later. A client is sometimes not ready to hear something that is true, so they might connect to your intuitive offering later on.
- Either way, remember to embrace a "take it or leave it" energy. If we assume a strong intuition is correct, we might push the client and later learn that the strong emotional sensation was connected to our own baggage. If you feel strongly, set it aside to reflect on it later.

Tips for listening beneath the surface and forming powerful questions:

1. Questions that seem too simple, obvious or silly, can sometimes evoke an ah-ha! Don't discount simple questions.
2. Sometimes, overcomplicated questions may seem powerful to us and just confuse the client.
3. Dropping one simple question can be more powerful than ten "intelligent overcomplicated questions."

4. Silence can turn an ordinary question into an extraordinary one. Silence allows the client to go beneath the surface and then keep going. If we move on too soon, we can accidentally bump back up to the surface.

Example: Ask one question at a time, count to ten. Trust. WAIT = "why am I talking?"

In conclusion, these are all very wonderful opportunities to listen beneath the surface, read between the lines and go deeper with our clients. Once we discover what's beneath the surface, we can invite new understanding, insights, and learning by helping our clients close the gaps to their success.

CLOSING GAPS & DISCREPANCIES

What happens when we are in a session and hear two conflicting stories from our client? How can we explore this without coming across as judgmental? Our clients can't fix what they don't see, so it is imperative to speak up if we see a discrepancy. In this segment, we explore how to navigate gaps and discrepancies masterfully.

For example:

"Laurel, I truly want to get this raise my boss keeps talking about!" Then, ten minutes later. "I refuse to talk to my boss."

"I heard that you have a list of positive reasons you are excited about getting divorced. I also saw tears and your energy drop. Can you share what the difference is?"

"You used the phrase, 'I love junk food and don't care if it is bad for me.' And now I'm hearing that deep down you are scared of a heart attack by the age of forty because it runs in your family. Would it help to dive deeper into the discrepancy here?"

These moments of discrepancy with your client are potential gold mines.

As a coach, you will see and hear discrepancies, assumptions or projections often quicker than the client. This is because you are not emotionally hooked to the problem. You are in a position to challenge the client to close these gaps.

Think of a gap. A gap means there is a here, and there is a there. There is a difference. Discrepancies are keen examples of gaps in our client's thinking. Inviting clients to dispel the gaps is the heart of inviting integration. Remember your client is a human being capable of abstract thought. All humans can get caught in the webs of fragmented thinking and illusions. These create the gaps that masterful coaches help close.

Below is a list of mindset pitfalls we all can fall into. We can't fix what we don't see, so these are important ways of thinking to catch and challenge in your client:

Assumptions	*Black / white thinking*	*Catastrophizing*
Exaggerating	*Generalizing*	*Justifications*
Minimizing	*Pessimistic thinking*	*Projecting*
Rigidity	*Self-depreciation*	

Possibilities exist 24/7/365. The question is: Does our client have access? Pitfalls, gaps, and internal blockages all limit access.

The problem is that when we have a negative, false, or limiting thought, the body reacts as if it is real, and this feeling leads us to believe it is real. This keeps us circling in the problem.

Access to possibility... denied.

Taking the client into their truth closes such gaps, connects them to their wholeness, and invites them to rise above the issues they face. When an illusion is brought to the surface for examination, the client can see it for what it is and it will fade.

Access... granted.

What can we do if our client is stuck in their story and can't seem to side step the problem? We can invite a pattern disrupt.

DISRUPTING A PATTERN

Did you know the brain can't be both in stress, in the problem, and creative? When a client gets stuck in the weeds, we help pull them out with a pattern disruption. The goal of a pattern disrupt is to interject something that stops the client from reeling in the problem to get back to being creative and coming up with more creative solutions.

What happens when a client talks in circles, feels passionate about their lack of options and is completely stuck in one perspective of their story? They become stuck in the obstacle.

As a coach, we help clients move from obstacle to opportunity.

For example, I could say, "I know this is going to seem random, but would you be willing to try something?" They say, "Sure." I invite them. "I invite you to pat your head and do a circle on your stomach at the same time. Can you do it?" If they are game to trying it, it could get them laughing. It could bring about a metaphor or take them back to a childhood memory. It also stopped the brain from circling.

Or, if a client is reeling in the problem and can't see out and we can ask, "I know this may seem off-topic, bear with me. What is your favorite hobby?" When they answer, the brain stops reeling and becomes curious. From there, I can inquire into parts of the hobby that are a success and see what translates to helping them with success in this area.

How about if a client is going on and on and we are getting nowhere fast. We can ask a question to interject a new thought pattern. For example, asking,

"What if you were a trapeze artist. What would you need to let go of to grab the next bar?" Once I asked this and it turned out my client laughed because she was afraid of heights. She said, "I wouldn't be a trapeze artist!" Even though the question didn't land for her, it offered a fun clearing so she could get back into creative thinking.

Or try this one out! The client is feeling the anger of their boss being disrespectful, and I say, "Can I invite you to do something? Let me know if it would help. What if you pretended the pillow you are sitting next to you was your boss and you allowed the two-year-old in you talk back to them?"

See what I mean? Pattern disrupts are left field! "Left field" is a baseball term. Wikipedia says, "Hits to left field tend to curve toward the left field foul line, and left fielders must learn

to adjust to that." Left-field questions or actions invite our clients to adjust, pay attention differently, and get the brain back into creative problem-solving.

In coaching, the goal is to locate solutions, and sometimes we need to invite a client to adjust their position to get there.

Pattern disrupting questions to consider:
- What is your favorite hobby?
- Who is the wisest person you know?
- What is your favorite color?
- What if this problem were an object. What object would it be?

Pattern-disrupting in somatics:
- Can you show me with your fist what this issue looks like?
- I invite you to stand up and shake the problem off.
- What if you grabbed this problem with your hands, rolled it up into a ball and set it to the side for a moment?

Somatics and Pattern Disruption

Guess what? Even though we have a fight or flight response, we very rarely physically fight someone or run away and flee in this day and age. When the brain perceives danger, it releases stress hormones. When adrenalin is released, it amps up the body's "sight, hearing, and other senses become sharper. Meanwhile, epinephrine triggers the release of blood sugar (glucose) and fats from temporary storage sites in the body. These nutrients flood into the bloodstream, supplying energy to all parts of the body." Harvard Medical (9)

What happens if we don't use the extra energy pumping through our system? We don't usually end up in an actual physical fight in this day and age, so it all stays put in our system.

In Chinese Traditional Medicine, our energy is called Chi. Chi represents the health of our energy and moving this energy is what keeps us healthy. The theory postulates that unmoved energy creates disease from stagnation. In Chinese traditions, there are practices of tai chi or chi gong. There are forms of chi cultivation that help us move and improve our energy and vitality.

We can invite our clients to move and use the energy in session. If they are really in a problem, we can invite them to "shake it off" or stand up and walk around. You may help a client create an energy reset. For example, if they are at work, can they close their office door and do five jumping jacks, hold a yoga pose, or anything that helps the stress hormones move along and process.

FRAMING CLIENT LEARNING

René Descartes was a French philosopher, mathematician, and scientist in the 1600s. His contribution to the world consisted of breaking things down into parts to understand them better.

Example: A frog can be a tree frog or a pond frog versus a toad. Also, Frogs have moist slimy skin, while toads have dry, bumpy skin.

Breaking things down into parts can help the client gain a visual understanding of a concept.

Example: Are you giving sympathy or empathy? Example: Items to Delegate - A List – B List – C List
In coaching, we help our client frame their solutions and new perspectives.

Framing also helps to connect dots, break down "parts," or understand connections more fully. Crafting a visual representation is a powerful way to frame.

Below are some examples:

My Responsibility	My Spouse's Responsibility
• Communicate my needs • Ask about concerns • Listen with an open heart	• Listen and reflect back • Empathize • Ask questions if unclear

When we give the client a visual to walk with, we help them move from the world of ideas into a vision with a tangible concept. Framing can be a fun, helpful, and creative approach. Some examples of items you can use for framing client ideas:

Arrows	*Balloons*	*Brick walls*	*Clouds*
Graphs	*Stars*	*Suns*	*Tables*
Targets	*Trees*	*Triangles*	*Umbrellas*

Below is an example of a client working on "not being pulled by distractions" and locating the things that help them rise above and stay more grounded in life.

The coach draws the outline, or invites the client to draw it and then the client fills it in.

THINGS THAT HELP ME RISE ABOVE

PULLS ME AT WORK PULLS ME AT HOME

THINGS THAT HELP ME STAY GROUNDED

With client's answers and added solutions:

THINGS THAT HELP ME RISE ABOVE
- hike on the weekend, church,
-attending my book club

PULLS ME AT WORK

- cell phone, office
door open for too long
I CAN:
- close my door, turn off cell

PULLS ME AT HOME

-kids not doing chores
- no dinner plans
I CAN:
-plan Sunday eve and
implement consequences

Coffee on the patio in the morning
Daily reflections/meditation
Walking the dog with my partner
THINGS THAT HELP ME STAY GROUNDED

Framing is a great way to outline the concepts the client is working towards. It can be fun and creative, or just a basic two-column graph. Framing offers client's structure so they can begin to visualize what the solution looks like. Happy framing!

CHAPTER FIVE
ℬ Coaching Program Frameworks ℭ

In a coaching session, the coach helps the client establish a clear agenda, or direction, for each session. In a coaching program, the coach helps the client identify the agenda for the entire scope of the coaching engagement.

It is common practice to offer a coaching program that supports clients to define and attain their goals. A program is an agreed upon amount of time that includes both structured and unstructured time.

In Chapter Five, we will cover the key ingredients for delivering a high-impact coaching program.

We will outline:

1. Considerations for creating meaningful Purpose & Outcomes statements.
2. Considerations for delivering self-assessments.
3. Ways to invite and facilitate action.
4. Ways to track the client's progress effectively.

FORMING A HIGH-IMPACT PROGRAM

In coaching, we come in as an equal partner. The client is responsible for their success and is the expert decision-maker for their life. The coach is responsible for the coaching container and is the expert in coaching. Remember, we may be an expert about external things, but we are never the expert of someone else's internal world. Forming a robust coaching engagement invites a long-lived relationship where we honor each phase of the client's unfolding. Long-term relationships occur when the client feels comfortable returning year after year and referring your services to others.

A coaching engagement is considered any longer-term commitment, or multiple sessions, by the client to engage in the coaching process. Engagements include a contract, coach/client agreements, and involve a program that the coach provides.

Professionals who do not create a solid partnership can end up with a "revolving door" practice. Do you want consistently need to go out and get new clients? Or, do you prefer to have returning clients and more referrals? A thriving practice means you have grown a community of clients you can form life-long relationships with. Below is an overview of the components for developing robust and lasting coaching engagements.

COACH / CLIENT RESPONSIBILITIES:

For the coaching to be a success, we each play a role. There is the coaching part of being a professional coach and then there is the business side of being a professional coach.

Coaching is such a unique approach, and you are such a unique individual that you will want to consider how you help teach the client how to get the most out of their time with you.

Yes, I said teach. The business side of coaching is about being business smart. Being business smart is about everything outside of a coaching session.

We are a coach in-session
and a business professional outside of a session.

When the client is taught how to get the most out of the coaching, they benefit. We can accomplish this by clearly outlining the responsibilities of each party.

• Define Coaching Scope	• Bring the agenda
• Confidentiality	• Advocate for needs in-session
• Transparency	• Advocate for needs out of session
• Bring all skills, talents, training	• Take-action
• Hold safe space	• Set realistic and clear goals
• Call out discrepancies	• Honesty with self and coach
• Keep client on topic	• Open/direct communication
• Be supportive, direct, and honest	• Show up on time
• Hold client accountable	• Communicate cancelations
• Show up on time	• Follow Program Agreements
• End sessions on time	• Ask questions if unclear
• Follow ICF Code of Ethics	

Some coaches will have the above list as a separate handout for their client or will review it together during the first session. Please adapt this list to your coaching practice as you see fit.

STAGES OF PARTNERING:

There are four stages of partnering. Each stage has its own unique needs and shifts the level of care.

Pre-Client:

Hi, my name is Laurel. Am I safe with you?

This is what your potential clients are wondering when they first connect with you. Before someone signs up with you, they need a way to get to know you and evaluate how safe you feel. Think about it. They are about to invest their time, energy, emotional safety, money, and future potentials with you. Coaching is a significant investment to them. Many coaches provide an opportunity for the potential client to feel heard, review what you do, and get a feel for how you care for them through the best business practice of offering a free coaching session or a free consultation.

In this stage, a person may come to you with questions like:
- Can coaching help me?
- Does coaching work?
- Will I be able to hold the coaching?
- What does the investment look like?
- Is the investment going to be worth my while?
- Is this person a good coach for me?

These are very normal questions percolating before someone will desire to move forward. It is important to have answers to the above questions thought-out in advance. Show up prepared to show your care and speak to each of these should they arise.

Caveat: If someone refers a potential client to you, there is less fear than if someone locates you online.

STEP ONE: Schedule the free session/consultation. STEP TWO: Email a Presession Questionnaire.
1. What is the overall situation you are seeking around?
2. What problem are you hoping to solve?
3. What are the implications if the problem is resolved?
4. What are you seeking from hiring a coach?

STEP THREE: Conduct the free call.

NAMING

You can give the free meeting a name. Some I have come across:
- Chemistry Call
- Discovery Call

o   Connection Call

o   Strategy Session

TIMING

If you are starting a new coaching business, giving a sample of coaching during your free call can be very helpful. After you have been in practice for a while, if you wish, you can transition to only doing a free consult without giving the coaching away for free.

FREE SESSIONS & CONSULTS: It is customary to offer a free call to a prospective coach. There are three common approaches.

- New Coach: When we are just starting out as a coach and building a new business, offering a complimentary coaching session can be beneficial. This session would be around 45-60 minutes. Setting aside an extra 15-20 minutes to discuss your program options after the session ends is helpful. This approach typically takes around 90 minutes total.
- Seasoned Coach: Seasoned coaches often offer a 60 minute call. 30 minutes coaching and 30 minutes for option review.
- Well Established Coach: A coach with a well-established practice can offer a 30 minute consultation without the sample coaching. In this approach, the coach asks the potential client a series of questions to see if they feel confident coaching will benefit.

You will want to choose the option that best fits your business model, experience level and your availability.

PROGRAM OPTIONS

The wonderful thing about a coaching practice is that you can set it up however you want. This can also be the hard part when getting starting. Here are some common approaches to help you craft your systems.

Program Launch – When clients are new to coaching, they choose how often to meet with you. In my experience, the following program offers will help them get the most out of their time with you:

- OPTION 1 – Weekly: This is an excellent option for goals with urgency.
- OPTION 2 – Tri-monthly: This option is excellent for high-priority goals that are non- urgent.
- OPTION 3 – Bi-monthly: Meeting twice a month is perfect for non-time-sensitive goals, general self-development support, and self-starters.

I do not recommend offering one-off sessions or once-a-month session options in the beginning of establishing a coaching program. Coaching is about progress and momentum. Meeting once a month makes it challenging to gain and sustain any momentum.

SESSION TIMING

You want to be clear on your session times. There are three common session time-frames: thirty (30) minutes, forty-five (45) minutes, and sixty (60) minutes.

Sixty-minute sessions are the most common. Once you become more seasoned at lasering in, you may decide to transition to thirty-minute sessions.

There is an unconscious time equation in our society that time = quality. In coaching, this is a false equation. It only takes one shift to get the client heading in a new direction. A shift entails a single change of perspective, like a trim tab on a boat. One shift invites an entirely new trajectory.

Ask yourself: What timeframe helps me be the best coach?

The answer may change over time. When I first started out, I was still learning how to laser in, and sixty minutes often didn't feel long enough. Years later, sixty minutes felt too long and thirty to forty-five minutes were perfect. The shorter sessions also got to the heart of the matter swiftly and invited the shift sooner.

The only right answer here is the answer that best supports you where you are at. When you are aligned with what you offer, the client will follow your lead on your process.

Efficiency Tip #1: It is beneficial to pad your scheduled time with 15 minutes on each end. Padding your schedule gives you time to transition between sessions, refuel and jot down any notes.

Efficiency Tip #2: As you take on more and more clients, you want to note how many sessions you can conduct in a single day and still maintain positive energy levels. Even extroverted coaches can burn out when they over-schedule. As an introvert, I would not schedule more than four sessions a day. I would space them out and I would not coach more than three days a week. Other coaches may coach up to five clients a day and four days a week. Find your rhythm and success formula.

FEE STRUCTURING
How do I set my fees?

This is a prevalent question for new coaches and has many answers. Here are some factors to consider to help you hone in on your fee structure as you grow.

The goal is to find a starting point and then raise your fees over time as you gain more experience and training.

Q: *Are you adding coaching to a business you already have in place as a consultant or counselor?*

If yes, you already have a background that includes working one-to-one with people or with teams. In these instances, it is common to start your coaching fees off higher. You may keep the fees you have already established with current clients. Or you may now increase your fees because of the value-add that coaching provides your practice.

Q: Are you starting your coaching business from scratch and new to having clients?

When starting a new coaching practice, it is common to start with lower fees to gain practice and build confidence.

Q: How much income do you need to make?

How much income we need can also drive our fee structure. Do the math and keep in mind your hourly rates also need to include outside of session time. Running a business means we have time contracting, budgeting, marketing, bookkeeping, etcetera. Reverse engineering what you need to live can help you find a reasonable fee rate to start at.

Keep in mind that no matter what your fees are, how confident you feel about your fees matters the most.

One coach charges $1,000 a month. She tells her potential clients, "I am not the cheapest, but I am one of the best." Your confidence in your fees helps a potential client feel safe to invest in your services.

Remember, coaching is a short-term investment with long-term results. The results clients get from coaching are with them for the rest of their life.

"What if the rest of your life
was the best of your life?"
~ Kobi Yamada

New Client:

WELCOME PACKET

In the Welcome Packet, place anything you will need them to have or know to get the most from their time with you. These items may include:

- Welcome Letter
- Coaching Agreement
- Coach / Client Responsibilities
- Booklist
- Session Prep Form

FOUNDATION SESSION

The first paid session is longer than the others. It can be ninety minutes or up to two hours, depending on what you wish to accomplish.

In this session, there may or may not be coaching yet, depending on how you wish to set it up. If your niche can have more urgent themes, the client may need their first interaction with you to have some laser coaching at the end so they can get an urgent need addressed. Consider what questions you want to ask so that you can be the best coach to them. Questions may vary greatly depending on the niche you serve.

Many coaches name the foundation session. For example, I call mine the "Get to Know You" session. The outline for your foundation session can depend on your niche. Below is a basic outline for a ninety-minute session. Please adapt as needed.

1. Personal Information gathering. (10 min)
2. Questions to get to know the client. (20 min)
3. Purpose & Outcomes for the coaching engagement. (15 min)
4. Assessment of situation (Wheel of Life, Wheel of Leadership, other) (20 min)
5. Review of Coaching Agreements and process. (10 min)

Active Client:

REGULAR SESSIONS

Meet as agreed for the program engagement they signed up for. I highly recommend scheduling a month in advance or finding a session time that doesn't change that often when possible.

At the end of the month, or their last session of each month, I check in with my clients and ask, "All right, so what are we doing next month? Same plan or shifting gears?" Then we schedule accordingly, and I bill at the beginning of the month for the agreed-upon scheduled sessions.

You will want to determine if you bill month to month or want to track packages. No matter how you set it up, be clear and transparent with how you work so the client can plan and knows exactly what to expect each step of the way.

EFFECIENCY TIP: It is best business practice in the coaching world to require pre-payment for sessions scheduled or anticipated. In other words, billing at the beginning of the month or charging upfront for a set amount of sessions. Receiving payment upfront saves you time and energy from tracking down payments after sessions have taken place.

PROGRESS ASSESSMENT

Coaching is about results. Conducting a progress assessment every three to six months is beneficial. A progress assessment is any follow-up to an initial assessment you conducted upfront.

These may include:
- Purpose & Outcomes
- Wheel of Life
- 8 Domains Assessment
- Enneagram: Levels of Development
- Enneagram: Transformations
- Other

MASTERY TIP: Follow up on Purpose and Outcomes every three months. Then conduct a more extensive progress assessment at the six-month mark. Your niche will determine the deeper dive assessment you choose to provide. The goal is always to go back and reassess progress.

GRADUATION SESSIONS

We graduate the client when they feel complete, or you observe they have accomplished what they came for and they agree. At this point, you can schedule a completion session.

You call it → The client has reached their goals and milestones.
They call it → They feel complete and satisfied.

You can create an outline for a graduation session or keep it organic. Here is a format to consider or adapt.

1. Review all progress to date. Celebrate!
2. Review growing edges: "What are your next steps to continue growth?"
3. Create a graduation plan together. A plan may include newly identified development points (see Eight Domains) or post-program goals established by the client. This way, the client has some valuable next steps to focus on. They will also know that they may come back into coaching for additional support in a different area or domain.
4. Offer maintenance options.

MAINTENANCE OPTIONS

After a client has completed their engagement, you may wish to offer one-off sessions or schedule "as-needed" sessions. It is advised to have a clear maintenance option ready to offer.

"Graduated" Client:

Graduating a client does not mean the relationship ends. Thriving businesses have systems to keep in touch and grow their community list so that they keep those relations alive and continue to nurture them.

GROW YOUR LIST

What would happen if your entire business and website were wiped out overnight so that nobody could find you? Yikes.

What if you kept a mailing list of all of your previous clients, potential clients, and community? Well, you can grow your business back in as little as one day and a few emails.

Keeping email lists of all clients, past and present, is imperative to success. Lists are the best way to avoid the revolving-door business approach that is exhausting.

Occasionally, clients complete their programs at the same time. When we keep a list, we can email everyone if we have a spot or two open up and then we get more clients in to fill those spots.

This is rewarding and much more effective than going out to locate new clients.

STAYING IN TOUCH

I have been surprised how many times I didn't stay in touch with past clients, I reached out to them years later, and they forgot to call me when a life blip happened. Even if a client has excellent results, years later, life gets busy, they get distracted and they forget you could be on their success team again. It is not personal.

Keep in touch. Every six months, do something to remind them you are there and that you still care. Staying in touch is also a great way to get more referrals. If a past client isn't in need, they may know someone who is.

Some ideas for staying in touch:
- o A free article or resource every six months
- o Newsletter or periodical
- o Birthday card or gift
- o Random phone call to say hi and check-in

- o A follow-up form: How did our coaching impact you six months later?
- o A free post-program session

ESTABLISHING PURPOSE & OUTCOMES

As mentioned earlier, there is an agenda for each session. The agenda for the entire coaching program is called the Purpose and Outcomes.

Purpose = Overall mission of your coaching program. It is written in paragraph format and includes the client's motivation for hiring you.

Outcomes = The specific goals that the client would love to accomplish in their time with you. These are 3-5 measurable and attainable.

I have found it much easier to start by helping the client identify their outcome statements first. Doing so will help illuminate the purpose statement by bringing it to life.

Below are examples of outcomes statements the client identified as the goals to accomplish in their coaching program.

Client A: (Emotional Eating)
1. Lose 20 pounds in 3 months.
2. Learn the difference between emotional hunger and true physical hunger.
3. Practice eating when I'm physically hungry at least three times a week.
4. Journal or call a friend each time I'm emotionally hungry and not physically hungry.
5. Learn how to identify my needs.

Client B: (Financial Freedom)
1. Get out of consumer debt by January 1st.
2. Read Dave Ramsey's book and start Baby Steps #1.
3. Have my first credit card paid off by March 1st.

4. Find five low-cost ways to be social and have fun.

5. Create a strategy w spouse to address emotional spending habits.

Outcomes statements are best when they follow the SMART goal method.
- Specific
- Measurable
- Actionable
- Realistic
- Timed

Once the client has gotten clear on the desired outcomes, their quantitative goals, it is time to invite the qualitative goals to surface.

This process can be as organic as you want it to be. You can invite the client to explore openly or give the purpose statement as a homework assignment.

If you enjoy a process to follow, below is a formula I've found to work wonders.

STEP ONE: Ask the client how their life will look and feel when they accomplish all of their outcomes. Make notes of keywords or phrases.

STEP TWO: Reflect back to them what you heard, using their words. You can plug their words into the following format if it helps.

It is my aim to: _____

So that I can: _____

As a result, I feel: _____

STEP THREE: Invite the client to comment and make adjustments.

Client A: (Emotional Eating)

It is my aim to break the cycle of the emotional eating cycle, gain peace with food and turn my "love/hate" relationship with food into one of love and self-care so that I can enjoy my health, my family, and my life. As a result, I feel lighter, vibrant, and healthy!

Client B: (Financial Freedom)

It is my aim to gain financial freedom, eliminate 100% of my consumer dept so that I can enjoy my life with my family and we will live abundantly with my spouse. As a result, I retire with more than enough left over to give back to charity.

CONCLUSION

After you have established clear goals and an inspirational statement, you have a reference point to refer back to as you begin the coaching program. Some clients will post their purpose statement where they will see it daily.

MASTERY TIP: It is common for clients to bring problems outside of the original purpose into their coaching program. For example, my client came to coaching and wanted help optimizing her health. She began showing up to sessions working on breakdowns with her boss.

You want to address this, just like you would in a session. I reflected back that this new topic has come up and invited her to consider if we needed to adjust her purpose and outcomes or return to the original purpose.

In truth, all growth can serve all areas of a client's life, especially when coaching to integration. However, it is good to reflect shifts in purpose that we observe so that the program stays in integrity and progress can be tracked.

In the above scenario, the client chose to create new purpose and outcomes for work and then return to the original purpose and outcomes once she handled the work issues.

DELIVERING SELF-ASSESSMENTS

Assessments provide data and shortcuts for the client's development. Assessments can be in-session or outside of the session. This segment will cover out-of-session assessments. In- session assessments are covered next under Exercises.

In coaching, all assessments are always "self-assessments" completed by the client and reflect the truth as the client is currently experiencing it.

Coaches do not assess the client or what is true for the client. We do observe and offer our observations so that the client can reflect and determine what is true for them. If you do

include any formal assessments in your coaching program, like Enneagram or MBTI, I invite you to look at the results through a purely coaching lens. Take the results as a "maybe" and a way to honor the client's current experience of their life and self.

Tips on Assessment Results:

- *Assessments reflect client experience and may or may not be the truth. This is OK; we want to know the client's experience because their experience eventually leads to their truth.*
- *Client-identified results help the client feel into truth and weed out illusion so that they can grow in their self-awareness.*
- *Behind the results is a person. Coach the heart of the person, not their results.*
- *Trust your client. If they disagree with the results, there is a reason.*

We want to use any assessments as feedback to help the client get clear on what will help them better define their goals.

Post assessment, you may ask your client questions like:

- "What would you like to do with these results?"
- "What about this process had meaning for you?"
- "What did you learn about yourself?"

OFFERING IN-SESSION EXERCISES

As we grow as a coach, our approach may become more dynamic. We may add in exercises within a session.

Types of exercises:
  1. *Experiential Exercises*

Experiential exercises can be anything from guided mediations to drawing or writing. An exercise is a guided experience offered by the coach. Exercises can be offered to help the client explore and journey towards their agenda.

You can also do framing exercises. Example: If the client is working on acceptance, you may have the client create three columns: can change, might change, can't change. Then invite them to fill in the blanks.

A well-designed exercise evokes the client's thinking to expand or become clearer. I recommend starting to grow your list of experiential activities.

Exercises can also be spontaneous. We will review a process for creating improvisational exercises with your client in the upcoming segment called "The Art of Framing."

  2. *Assessment-Based Exercises*

Assessments are excellent tools for client self-awareness and integration. Assessments may take a little longer in sessions because they can invite rich conversations around self- awareness. Assessments can also be a quick way to help a client locate blind spots. If an assessment is overly involved or a standard part of your coaching program, you can also assign an assessment as homework and invite the client to bring their results to the next session.

Below are assessments for client integration:

- StrengthsFinder 2.0
- Emotional Intelligence 2.0
- Enneagram - Levels of Development
- Enneagram - Transformations
- Values Inventory
- MBTI / DISC / Enneagram

3. *Stress-Reduction Exercises*

The brain can't be both creative and under stress. Offering to start the session with a de- stress exercise acts as a pattern disrupt and helps the client get the most from the session.

Here are two great examples:

"Shake It Off" – Invite the client to stand, take deep breaths, and shake off whatever stress came with them for the week or from the day.

"Calming Down" – Invite the client to get centered in their seat. Take a deep belly breath in and smile on the exhale while making an "ahhhh" sound. Smiling shifts the brain from stress hormone release to oxytocin release. Have them do these three times. Repeat if needed.

Exercise Best Practices:

- Ask permission to offer an exercise. For example, if the client is in the middle of a meaningful stream of thought, they may say no so they can finish processing. It is important to honor them.
- Keep spontaneous exercises short and sweet. Longer exercises take away from client time. Of course, if a longer exercise is a part of your coaching program, then you can be clear with your client about what to expect.
- After any exercise is offered, turn it back over to the client. Check in and ask how the activity impacted them.

INVITING ACTIONS & HOMEWORK

In a purist coaching model, the coach helps clients formulate their homework, tasks, and actions.

In integrative coaching, we honor the client first and then make offers that invite integration and development. The integration of coach/client wisdom helps the client discover possibilities they may not have discovered on their own.

There are three primary types of homework we can offer to the client:

Exercises:
An exercise is a single assignment. A one-time exercise is a great way to help the client create a new experience, experience a challenge or try out a new perspective or approach.

Example: Call around to price different options before deciding.

Practices:
A practice is an ongoing activity. Practices may have timeframes, like two weeks, or may be open-ended. Practices help us cultivate a new awareness, ingrain a positive new habit, or explore new potentials.

Example: Sit with your cat by the window every day for five minutes. Relax and enjoy the moment, in the now.

Self-Observations:
Self-observation is an invitation to gain self-awareness, locate blind spots, and discover what is life-affirming for the client.

My mentor Sandy called this "Catch yourself in the act of..." Noticing what is going on when you are in a pattern or having an issue come up.

Example: Catch yourself in the act of blurting out too soon. What was the circumstance? How did you feel after? How did you perceive the impact on others? What other option would you prefer?

Homework Best Practices:
- Client goes first to design their next actions and tasks.
- If you observe a growth opportunity, you may offer a homework assignment designed to inform the client's path to development.
- A masterful coach embodies a "take it or leave it" attitude by giving the client the option to take on the homework if it speaks to them or to leave it if it does not.
- Be careful to not "overfeed" the client. Offer homework that is doable and attainable. When we want the client to get results, getting overzealous with homework can be tempting. Consider the context of your client's time and capacity to follow through. One well-purposed homework assignment is better than ten.

TRACKING CLIENT PROGRESS

There are a variety of options for client progress tracking and tracking your coaching hours. Below are some considerations.

What is the best form of tracking?

That is a trick question. The answer is: The one you will use!

I am very accustoming to freak-out moments where a colleague calls and says, "Help, I've gotten behind on tracking my hours and can't find my CCEs to renew my credential!"

Getting into the habit of tracking makes credentialing and re-credentialing much smoother.

Tracking client progress can depend on what level you wish to be involved. Some coaches leave all client progress completely up to the client to track. Others keep copious notes to refer back to. I trust you will formulate a process that works best for you. Below is a happy medium that I've seen work wonders.

PROGRESS TRACKING SIMPLIFIED:

STEP ONE - For each client, create a single Word or Google document. Add these categories:

- Client Name
- Start Date
- Tools Covered
- (anything else immediately helpful, like Personality Type)

STEP TWO - Track each session by placing the following:

- Session Date
- Takeaways
- Homework

STEP THREE – Repeat. Add the current session to the top of the page. For example:

- 6/15/21
  o (highlights of takeaways / homework)
- 6/1/21
  o (highlights of takeaways / homework)
- 5/20/21
  o (highlights of takeaways / homework)
- Etc.

This simplified tracking method allows you to glance at the overview quickly, recall where you left off, and important considerations for this client.

One day my client showed up and said he didn't know what to work on. He felt like he was in a great spot with his progress. Instead of assuming there was nothing to work on, I asked him if he would like to do a session review. He agreed that would be great. I pulled up his Client Overview and we recapped a few of the past sessions. Once we began this process, an immense underlying fear came up for him, and the session ended up being one of the most profound sessions. The overview helped us efficiently hit on key points. This overview is also helpful so that you don't have to rely on memory.

When I began coaching full time, keeping track in my head of which tools I had introduced to which clients became harder and harder. This quick list at the top of the page allows you to recall what tools have been covered so that you can refer back to them in a session as needed.

The overview can also act as a backup when you are going back to document coaching hours completed. It is a great way to record.

Happy highlighting!

CALCULATING THE RETURN ON INVESTMENT (ROI)

Anytime we use a scoring system, or coaching self-assessment, we have the opportunity to track the return on investment for our client. The most simple and popular scoring system is a scale from one to ten, one being the lowest and ten representing the highest.

Some examples are:
- Wheel of Life – Have the client score their level of happiness in each area of their life.
- 8 Domains – Have the client score their proficiency in each domain.
- Purpose & Outcomes – Have the client score how close they are to attaining each outcome.
- General coaching questions – Have the client rate an area of improvement. Example: Confidence.

For example, if the client is working on confidence, and I ask upfront: "On a scale from one to ten, where is your confidence level now?" They score a four. Then we can rescore after coaching for a while. With the new data point, you can do the math and inform them of the actual percentage of their improvement. (The formula to follow is included below.)

You can also use this to track specific goals. One example is Enneagram Transformations. Help the client identify the top three transformations to work on. Have them score each using the one to ten scale. After coaching for a while, rescore and see what percent they moved.

A reasonable timeframe for rescoring is every three to six months, depending on how you structure your coaching program.

The Three-Step ROI Formula:

STEP ONE: What is the difference? The below example is based on a scoring of 1-10. 10 being highest and 1 being lowest.

- My client scored themselves on their confidence levels at a 3 out of 10.
- When they rescored themselves six months later, the rating went up to a 7 out of 10.
- The difference, or increase, was 4. (7 − 3 = 4)

STEP TWO: Divide the increase by the original number.

- $4 \div 3 = 1.333$

STEP THREE: Multiply the resulting number by 100.

- $1.333 \times 100 = 133\%$

RESULT: This client, over a six-month period, saw a 133% increase in their confidence.

CHAPTER SIX
๛ Coaching to Wholeness ๛

In Chapters One through Five, we looked at the foundational approaches and skills for success. In the following chapters, we will look at what it takes to up-level your coaching skills, processes, and coaching presence.

We will now take some deeper dives. We will explore how to take your clients into their wholeness so that they can cultivate awarenesses that lead to integration.

In Chapter Six, we pave the path to understanding what it means to coach a client from their wholeness. We explore mastery, the milestones to look out for, how to help your client locate their true self and shed their false self.

We will also cover frameworks to help your client be guided by their core values, live aligned with their personal power, and how to manage their time and energy.

We will wrap up the chapter by looking at perspectives that elevate a client's emotional intelligence and how to help support your client through a variety of rough patches.

INVITING THE MASTER
One of my passions is to bridge ancient wisdom to modern-day challenges. One such wisdom tradition passed down for centuries is found in ancient Toltec teachings around self- mastery.

The Toltecs speak to the stages of human development and offer a path to view our potential from. They call these stages "The Victim," "The Warrior," and "The Master." These terms are metaphorical states of empowerment that represent the path of integration.

Now, let's look at the empowering perspective the teachings offer us and what these lessons teach us about coaching our clients.

"THE VICTIM"

The Toltecs teach us that we naturally depend on our parents' or guardian care when we are born and throughout early childhood. We remain dependent on others for safety, food, and shelter for years. Early childhood dependency is a normative human experience.

It is one thing to be biologically dependent on another for our life and care, and it is another thing to remain dependent after the need for dependency has passed. If we choose not to take a stand for our life and remain dependent, we stay in a disempowered state. The Toltecs refer to this state as the "victim."

While we grow chronologically, we grow from no choice about our physical dependence into choice. Once we become capable of tying our shoelaces, brushing our teeth, dressing on our own, and making ourselves food, we have a choice about whether we remain emotionally, mentally, and spiritually dependent on those around us. Our happiness becomes more of a coin toss if we become entangled in this stage too long.

In modern-day psychology, we know growing out of the state of dependence as "individuation." When we individuate from our parents, we gain a sense of our self, independent of others. We begin to locate our center of personal power. The Toltecs refer to the process of stepping into our power as the "warrior."

THE WARRIOR

As we get older, we can start to meet our own needs and individuate from our caretakers. We can take a stand from our personal beliefs and step into the warrior part of ourselves. In warrior, we take a stand for who we are, what we want/don't want, and begin to live with a vision of our own creation.

The Toltecs teach that we can become stuck in this stage, even throughout adulthood. In this stage, we fight, push and react against life. Warrior isn't always easy, and in adulthood, we may slip back into a victim role, consciously or unconsciously. Others may become hardened and continue to fight against life.

The Toltecs invite us to step out of fighting, not regress into the victim role and realize there is a difference between growing up and waking up.

The Toltecs invite us to develop our responsiveness to life, see a bigger picture, become self- aware and increase our human capacity for virtue. They call this growth the "master."

THE MASTER

When we move beyond warrior, we begin to quest for a bigger picture, healthier and more empowered options, and a brighter future. We start to see life integratively, and we include all aspects of life, including death, joy, and sorry. We see what is and choose our response to what is. We dispel the illusions of limitation. We move from fear to love, from vice to virtue.

As we move into mastery, we begin to see inner-connectivity and live life with our legacy in mind. We use our life for service and purpose. We learn from our own potential.

Victim → *Warrior* → *Master*

We often think of "master" as someone enlightened, sitting quietly and meditating on a hilltop for years on end. Yet, if a child is being abused, then there is a time for the master to take a stand and step back into warrior to be of service to the well-being of another.

When our clients come to us, they are no longer dependent on their parents. They may be in warrior or toggle between warrior-master. Many are tired of fighting for things in life and are ready to invite life from a higher perspective and masterful vantage point.

Our job as a coach is to invite the master to come forward. To do this, let's look at the stages of development and their correlating capacities:

STATE of BEING	QUALITY of LIFE	RESULTING LIFE EXPERIENCE
Victim	Dependence	Low to no capacity for self-agency.
Warrior-Victim	Fights - Lives as "I"	Capacity for self-agency develops. Push energy is tiring.

Warrior-Master	Invites – Lives as "We"	Capacity for self-agency expands. Relational energy is inspiring. Productive outcomes are inviting.
Master	Sees - Lives through "All"	Full awareness of the bigger picture. Lives with wisdom of all that is.

Until we take a stand for ourselves, we will remain a victim, even into adulthood. Taking a stand from a victim perspective is to fight against life. Stepping into master, we rise above life's strife and invite things to go right.

When life needs us to take a stand, the question is: Are we taking the stand from victim- warrior or master-warrior?

MASTERY

Mastery is not just for Buddhist monks or ninjas. Integration is not only for the enlightened. We all have the capacity to become masterful and elevate our potential. Mastery also does not equal perfection.

Perfection is an illusion in this crazy big world of relativity. Being sentient means we have awareness and choice. We can choose to react to life through fear, hurt, or anger, or respond to life with a bigger picture awareness. We have the choice to evoke the human virtues that are missing, like compassion or integrity.

Mastery does not mean that our life becomes perfect. There is a Zen saying, "Before enlightenment, chop wood, carry water. After enlightenment, chop wood, carry water."

Life will continue to be what it is, both messy, painful, joy-filled, and amazing. Mastery doesn't eliminate devastation, but it can minimize it.

Living masterfully means we return to the wholeness within and develop our full capacity. This Cherokee legend speaks of a grandfather teaching his son about the choice to develop:

"There are two wolves
within us all, always at battle.
The first is anger, fear, arrogance, guilt.
The second is love, joy, benevolence, truth."
"Which one will win?" asks the grandson.
"The one you feed."

How can we tell when the coaching is working and our client is becoming more and more masterful? There are three milestones to look out for.

OBSERVING THE THREE MILESTONES

How can we tell when the coaching is working, the client is integrating, and their potential has elevated? There are three observable milestones we can see our clients reach. Each builds off of the next.

MILESTONE ONE: Self-Awareness

Self-awareness is "conscious knowledge of one's own character, feelings, motives, and desires." - Google Dictionary

In my early 20s I struggled with emotional eating. If I got stressed out, bored, or felt depressed, I would turn to food for comfort. As I started to face this about myself, I started gaining self-awareness.

At first the eating just seemed like a reaction and it was. As I got more in touch with my motivation, I would catch myself and realize, "I am not physically hungry right now. I'm feeling tired and needing rest, not sugar."

Once I leveled up my self-awareness, I began healing this pattern in my life. A pattern that left me feeling stuck, powerless, and out of control.

We can't fix what we don't see. Self-awareness is key to all other mastery in one's life. It is the prerequisite to all growth and development. For this reason, it is Milestone #1.

1. We can see demonstrations of self-awareness when we observe our clients:
2. Recognizing their motivations (beneath a behavior).
3. Readily separate fact from fiction.
4. Notice their true self and can say no to the false self.
5. Move from living at the effect of their life to living at the cause.
6. When asked how they feel or think, they can answer.

If clients are not self-aware when they begin coaching, they are in self-discovery mode, which is a sign to stay put with self-awareness questions.

Self-awareness has three base layers to it:

1. Emotional – How aware is my client of their feelings?
2. Somatic – How aware is my client of their physical reactions?
3. Intellectual – How aware is my client of their mindsets, beliefs, values, and strengths?

Once a client becomes self-aware, this naturally leads to the next milestone.

MILESTONE TWO: Self-Generating

Self-awareness naturally helps us to become self-generating.

When we become self-generating, we generate answers from within, "rather than by some external force". – Google Dictionary

There is an underlying distinction that it is helpful to be aware of here. It is one thing to self- generate; it is another thing to self-generate in the right direction… *towards our goals.*

One of my very first coaching experiences was with my mentor Sandy. I was in coaching because I was going through life as a single mom struggling to make life work. I remember a coaching moment with her that shifted me forever. I was beating myself for mistakes I had made. I think I said something along the lines of, "I can't believe I made so many dumb choices."

She said, "Did you choose those paths?" I said, "Well, yes. Nobody else made those choices but me." I had a "well duh, of course" attitude.

She said, "Interesting. Did you really choose, or did you react at the moment?" This stumped me. I had reacted. I didn't choose. I learned not choosing is also a choice. It is a choice to not pause, reflect, align with my truth, and then decide what the best choice is. All of my "mistakes" boiled down to an unconscious string of reactions. I was living at the effect of my life, not at the cause.

I guess you could say I was self-generating but in very misaligned ways that, looking back, left me regretful.

In coaching, we want to ensure we are generating towards our goals. A Course in Miracles has a lot to say about living empowered:

> *"Can you see how all misery stems*
> *from believing you are powerless?"*
> *A Course in Miracles*

Self-generation is the second milestone because it takes self-awareness to help determine if we are heading in the correct trajectory, the direction we would choose for ourselves.

We can see demonstrations of self-generation when we observe our clients:
1. Ideas and insights come from within.
2. Inner guidance develops.
3. Solutions are more evident.
4. Ability to take a step back and reflect on what is *really* true.

5. Actions are intrinsically motivated.

6. Criteria for choice becomes about alignment with core values.

Once a client becomes self-generating towards their goals, this naturally leads to the next milestone.

MILESTONE THREE: Sustains Success

Self-generation naturally helps us to sustain our success.

A client of mine came into coaching wanting to make peace with her family. We started out working on self-awareness. What was true/what wasn't? How was she feeling? What was she needing? What did she value?

Six months later she was still having family issues. She said, "I don't feel as if I'm making any progress." I had observed her progress; however, when the success isn't yet to Milestone 3, it can feel to the client as if they haven't succeeded yet.

I used the 3 Milestones to reflect back to her what I observed. I said, "When you first came to coaching, I would ask you a question and many times the response was "I'm not sure." In the last three months I've asked you questions and you not only have an answer, you have powerful insights coming through. I've observed you have become 1) self-aware; and 2) self-generating. What do you think about this?"

I turned it back over to her to see if she felt the same way.

She lit up! She agreed that she had noticed that difference as well. I then gave a brief overview of the three milestones and said, "The good news is that sustainable success comes next."

She began using her self-generation at family gatherings and with her spouse. She began to shift her relationship to the dynamics at play, dynamics she felt were dysfunctional and triggered her to react in a dysfunctional way. She began to choose her responses. She chose compassion, respect, and love. After a while, she reported that her relationship with her husband, kids, and extended family was going well. Not just once but each time they had a gathering.

Milestone 3 is reached when success becomes sustainable.

We can see demonstrations of sustainability when we observe our clients:
1. Replicate successes despite new challenges that arise.
2. Overcome obstacles as they come up.
3. Unhook self-fulfilling prophecies.
4. Break out of patterned ways of being and become responsive.
5. Overcome inner obstacles as they arise.
6. Address fears of failure and of success in real-time.
7. See how shifting the perspective, shifts the outcome.

SUMMARY

These three milestones are the behind-the-scene goals of integrative coaching.

We are helping our clients reach these peaks so that they can make it to the top of their potential. These milestones are observable and confirm progress.

Milestone 3 is also how we "graduate" the client from the program they started with. Once they have reached sustainable success, they may wish to switch gears and work on another aspect of their life.

As you are coaching, notice what milestone a client is at and honor that. If they are working on self-awareness, stay with them in that. Once they become self-generating, step back and see what they come up with so that they can eventually walk away with sustainable outcomes and thank you for walking this path with them on their journey.

EMBRACING WHOLENESS

You are whole and complete as you are. Your clients are whole and complete as they are. You have everything you need to succeed. Your clients have everything they need to succeed.

When we embrace who we are, it becomes much easier to release what we are not. When we embrace our wholeness, it becomes much easier to amplify our personal power. Can you recall your favorite, most inspiring vacation? I'm curious. What made this vacation so inspiring and memorable for you? I imagine you had loads of fun, created meaningful memories, or felt a connection. I can imagine you can list a few inspiring moments in your life. What do you think was the deeper reason behind inspiring moments like these?

I'll offer a suggestion. You see if it fits. Were these inspired moments experiences that were heart-filled? Moments experienced without the ego? Did you experience life as whole? A vacation is an example of an opportunity to leave our defense mechanisms at the door and live in pure enjoyment. When we coach, help your client locate their bliss, heart, and spirit of what moves them!

What would happen if people started living through their wholeness? What would it feel like to lead life through wholeness? It feels solid, confident, calm, honest, alive, natural, and fulfilling to me. How about you?.

CONSIDER: Current self-development models teach us to take who we are today and begin developing from there. There is nothing wrong with the current approach. All development can benefit. Yet, this linear approach can only get us so far. In integrative coaching, we are introduced to our highest self, and then we have our wholeness inform our development.

Huge difference!

The first perspective gets us only this far: _____→

The highest self gets us this much farther: _____→

This is because the ego cannot solve the problems of the ego.

You might be wondering what this has to do with wholeness? Consider: How do we help our clients locate their highest self? We invite them to experience their wholeness.

Where is your coaching mastery located? In your wholeness. This quote is exemplifies the power of this concept:

> *"You have taught [yourself] what you are.*
> *You have yet to allow what you are teach you."*
> *A Course in Miracles*

Our wholeness is always there for us. It never goes away. It may feel unreal or absent when we are under duress. Wholeness is like the sun. The sun is always shining. Clouds can block it, but once the clouds pass, the sun shines yet again.

The question remains… If we are whole and complete as we are, why are we not perfect? Why are our reactions not perfect? Why do we not always feel complete? Why would we need coaching?

Our success is embedded in what we are. Yet, we often begin living through what we aren't. This is the human plight and hero's journey to return to the wholeness within. It is good to note that when stress hits, it is easy to become self-forgetting. Even the most developed person can slip back into old patterns.

Wholeness seems so far away during hardship. Yet, it is always right here within each of us, ready to be accessed, felt, and lived through. Part of masterful coaching is taking the client back into their wholeness, reminding them of their wholeness and inviting them to come home to themselves. Your clients may come to coaching never having considered experiencing their life through their wholeness. You get to introduce them. What an honor.

LOCATING THE TRUE SELF

If we are to evolve, it is but illusions we must resolve.

Temet nosce is the Latin phrase for "know thyself." According to the Greek writer Pausanias, temet nosce became a guiding maxim. It was inscribed at the Temple of Apollo at Delphi. The phrase originated from ancient Kemet, where many of the philosophers studied and were inspired to think in new ways.

How does coaching empower the client to *know thyself?*

Remember, your clients are not their fears. Your clients are not their defense mechanisms. Your clients are not their limiting beliefs.

How then do we understand who our client really is, at their core? How do we see them through their potential? How do we help them see their true self? We can start by understanding what we are *not* in order to start weeding through the false from the true.

What we are *not* is anything that stems from fear or arrogance, the two egoic imbalances. What we *are* is embedded in our gifts, potentials, and core values. From these we can extend any human virtue if we choose.

We will never extend the virtue of love while living in defense. We will never extend the virtue of humility while living a façade.
We will never extend the virtue of compassion while living in judgment.

We will never experience the spirit of courage while living in cowardice. We will never experience the spirit of patience while living with push.

We will never experience the spirit of generosity while living in avarice.

When we live through the true self, we live at the level of cause. When we live through fears, reactions, and defenses, we live through strands of effects. To live at the level of cause, we must first be aware of which foundation we are standing in. Truth or illusion. True self or false. Self-knowledge or self-deception.

Truth is causative and positive.
Illusions are elusive and intrusive.

Self-Knowledge - I am aware of my wholeness -	Self-Deception - Inner-doubt fragments my awareness -
Am I living through?	Do I get blocked by?
⅄ My core values	⅄ Triggers
⅄ My natural strengths & gifts	⅄ Fears / anxieties
⅄ My potentials	⅄ Reactivity
⅄ My "Genius Zone"	⅄ Negative emotional states
⅄ Awareness of my hard-wiring	⅄ Illusory thinking / inauthenticity
⅄ Awareness of the false-self	⅄ Perceived limitations
⅄ Confidence in my purpose here	⅄ Pushing against life
⅄ Confidence in self	⅄ Withdrawing from life
⅄ Choice of who I want to be	⅄ Arrogance
⅄ Self-worth	⅄ False beliefs

Life is first about finding our true self. Life can go beyond finding ourselves. Life can also be about choosing to create who we wish to be.

Self-awareness is the bridge from the false to the true.

Your heart is your lantern bridging you
from the false to the true.

How can we help our clients navigate all of their parts and separate the false from the true? That question is answered as we understand the depth of self-identify.

UNDERSTANDING SELF-IDENTITY

How we self-identify directly impacts all areas of our life. Our clients come to us to accomplish goals and gain new skills. One of the ways we help them reach their aims is by inviting self-examination. Is who they are showing up as, who they wish to be?

Understanding the role of self-identity in the coaching process will help inform your mastery as a coach. Your client has different parts to their identity. We are now going to explore the nature of human identity so that you can help your clients step into their full capacities.

As we grow chronologically, we gain experiences. These experiences expand into a variety of aspects of self. In my 20s, I became a wife, a mother, a manager, and a painter. Those became facets of who I was. Other parts of self we have are cultural, environmental, our hardwiring, and the messages we were raised with.

As we become more self-aware, we have the opportunity to examine the aspects of self. Some aspects reflect the true self and some reflect the false. Self-awareness allows us to choose which parts to embrace, which parts to grow, and which parts to let go. The beauty of choice is that you get to decide. To keep false aspects of self feels safe. There are reasons they are there. Yet, the inauthentic parts we have accumulated over time keep us the most limited.

Our ego has the most parts. These parts represent the false self, defenses, facades, masks we wear.

Our wholeness also has parts. These parts are extensions and expressions of our true self, our gifts, values, passions, and purpose. In integrative coaching, we help our clients become aware of their parts to remove the false, amplify the true, and see their way through.

Your client's wholeness and all extensions of their wholeness elevates their human potential.

PARTS OF SELF:

Here are some parts to start examining:

- Age	- Experiences	- Ideals	- Spiritual beliefs
- Career	- Family messages	- Mindsets	- Social preferences
- Culture	- Fears - Passions	- Status	

- Disadvantages	- Gender	- Personality	- Strengths
- Ethnicity	- Gifts	- Physical attributes	- Super powers
- Environment	- Habits	- Privileges	- Titles
- Education	- Hobbies	- Qualities	- Values

In coaching, we can inquire about parts to help our clients engage parts that empower them and shed parts that are hindering. "What part of you is answering this question?" "What part of you is afraid?" "Who do you need to be to make this a reality?" "What part of you can say yes?" "What part of you says no?" Working on our parts is an empowering process. Once we identify our parts, we can evaluate if they are serving us or swerving us.

ONTOLOGICAL EXPLORATIONS
on·tol·o·gy

/än'täləjē/

noun

1. the branch of metaphysics dealing with the nature of being.
2. a set of concepts and categories in a subject area or domain that shows their properties and the relations between them.

   – Oxford Languages

Just like we have a part of us that is an inner-critic and a part that is our highest self, the problems we help our clients solve also have parts. The universe is made up of the macro and the micro. If we stay in the big picture, we miss the details. If we ruminate and overthink, we can get stuck in analysis paralysis.

Descartes was a philosopher known for scientifically breaking things down in order to better understand them. We see how his techniques around compartmentalization are still with us today. In universities, all departments are separate: mathematics, science, psychology, medical, etcetera. (20)

Compartmentalizing is an asset when we need to break something down to better understand the parts. Yet, it can become a liability when we forget that these parts are interconnected to a greater whole and we get trapped in linear approaches.

When I was in junior high, I was under a lot of stress. I got in a fight with the most popular girl in school and she turned a lot of my friends against me, and this clique also loved to bully. I dreaded waking up in the morning unless it was a weekend. During this time, I also thought I had a heart condition. My heart wouldn't stop pounding or palpitating. My mom took me to the doctor. He looked at me, listened to my symptoms, and outright asked, "Are you under any stress?"

I burst out crying. He nodded and said I was fine and reassured me I'd be OK. My heart issue was stress-induced. This doctor was integratively informed. He saw the bigger cause and effect, beyond his allopathic training.

Some call this out-of-the-box thinking. I call this reality.

In coaching, we help the client break things down into parts. Parts help us review what is true, what is false, what is blocking, and what is empowering.

The client is feeling overwhelmed: "What part of this is easy to manage?"
The client is thinking negatively: "What part of this has a silver lining?"
I'm self-coaching and feeling worried: "What part can I say yes to?"
I come to coaching upset, and my coach asks: "What is going well?"

Creating distinctions, examining all angles, helps our clients weed through the details to help locate the helpful, positive, or open aspects of the experience they are having.

Now let's circle back to engaging the wholeness of our clients. Let's help them learn who they are and what they are capable of. We illuminate the path by helping our clients identify and live through their Core Values.

IDENTIFYING CORE VALUES

"Wow. That person is a complete jerk!" said my teenage son after he got cut off in traffic. Why was he upset?

The answer is found in human behavior.

When we are upset by an event or a choice someone made, our own upset reflects back to us something we deeply value. If you didn't value it, you wouldn't be upset. One aspect of who we are, the true self, is made up of our core values. The theory that Dr. Marshall Rosenburg posited is that our core values generate our personal needs.

Core values represent a central theme in our lives and if they do change, we are slow to change them. Whereas needs shift daily, are situation based and reflect back to us our core values.

Understanding our core values is a big leap in self-awareness and self-understanding. If I know I value respect, I can then realize, "No wonder I'm upset by every little thing the kids move in the house without asking. I see it as disrespect."

Core values also reflect back our own value. That is right, our personal value is brought to life as we align with our values. Our self-worth, our values, and the myriad virtues that are already alive within us grow as we come to embrace the full spectrum of our humanity. We have the capacity for such a wide variety of human virtue. These virtues within us are expressions of the value we can bring forth in any situation we choose. What do you wish to be the possibility of? You get to choose the human virtue you engage in any situation.

In Hyrum Smith's book, *The 10 Natural Laws of Time and Life Management*, he points out in law #3 that "When your daily activities reflect your governing values, you experience inner peace." He talks about how even if we go through utterly stressful situations or immense challenge, we can still experience inner peace because we are aligned on the inside.

I had the opportunity to experience this law firsthand when I endured a mutiny. Yes, an actual mutiny. The Oxford dictionary defines a mutiny as "An open rebellion against the proper authorities."

When I was initially promoted to Director of Education, the school owner had also hired on a new president to run the school. The new president had no background in running a school. Safety and trust were broken early on. I would show up for work and field complaint after complaint. I was up against a wall. The owner did not want to hear about any issues and brushed them off. After complaints of emotional harassment and intimidation, my values for protection and integrity began to rise to the surface.

I took the upper hand and issued a school-wide survey, "How are we doing?" It was confidential; one other staff member and I would type the results so nobody could fear retaliation. Best practices. The complaints were off the charts. The degree of complaints people shared when they felt safe due to confidentiality promised was very eye-opening. The typed results were shared openly with everyone, including the president and the board.

The president came into my office, closed my door and demanded to see the written submissions. I refused and stuck to my integrity. I also value being protective. The students were promised confidentiality, and I was going to keep it that way. He proceeded to go through my files while I sat there. I informed him the written copies had been taken off campus. He left, threatened my job, and called the owner to insist I be fired immediately. I thought, "Well, if I lose my job, at least I did the right thing." Looking back, I could not have done it any other way. My value for integrity wouldn't allow it, even if my position was placed on the line.

The next day, I was asked to leave.

When the staff, faculty, and students got wind that the results came in, were ignored, and the administrator they could trust was let go, they coordinated a full-blown boycott of the school.

No one showed up for classes except the owner's wife.

The community culture was one of justice and respect. When equity was breached, the community aligned with their values, and they took a stand. On day two of the boycott, the board convened, and I was offered my job back with a promotion. The president was let go.

Having been coaching since 2005 and learning the power-packed within our own values, I'm surprised how many people live life without any awareness of their core guiding values.

In coaching, helping our clients identify their core-guiding values is critical to empowerment and is intimately interwoven with understanding our self-worth.

How do we help our clients identify their core values? There are many paths to the top of the same mountain. This process is helpful and can be completed within one session or as a homework assignment.

IDENTIFYING CORE VALUES

To identify core values, we use a process called a value sort:

1. Answer the questions that reflect your values.
2. After writing down all the values your experiences reflect, notice any duplicates.

3. Group: Create five columns. Which values are connected to each other? Place these in groups together.

   a.   Some values may show up in multiple groups.

   b.   Example Column 1: compassion, spirituality, integrity, love.

   c.   You may only fill the first three columns, that is OK. Fill three minimum, five max.

4. Review each column and ask, "Which one of these do I need to come first so the others may be supported?" Circle that one.

   a.   Example: Column 1: If "love" comes first the rest of the values are fully supported, so I circle "love."

5. The values circled are considered the core values.

Note: There is no one "truth" for these. Everyone's answer will be unique, and this is excellent. If we all valued the same thing, other things that are important would not get tended to. We all play a role. We are all of value.

COACHING TO CORE VALUES

Once we help clients identify core values, it becomes evident where their values are showing up and not showing up.

Values can also help guide us when life gets stressful, like getting fired after a mutiny. Dr. Steven Covey speaks of values as the lighthouse on the rock, guiding our ship safely to shore during a storm. I couldn't agree more.

Once the client has values to return to, we can help them relate to their inner-critic and highest self. Here is how.

UNVEILING THE INNER-CRITIC & HIGHEST-SELF

Oh, the inner-critic!

We all have one, clients and coaches alike. The inner-critic goes by different names such as monkey mind or saboteur. It is the voice of our egoic self, armed and ready to self- deprecate, evaluate, plop us into depths of fear and compare our lives against others.

One way to address the inner-critic in a coaching relationship is to have fun with it. Give it a name, a color, draw it out as a symbol. Once it is named, you and the client have a frame of reference and language around the critic. You may even hear your client laugh at themselves. "Oh, there goes my darn "False Alarm" again!"

Bringing levity into the mix helps the client not to take their inner critic so seriously. After all, its meanderings are based on illusions anyway.

To have some fun and creativity with your client ask them to identify:
1. How does the inner-critic feel?
2. What does it love telling me?
3. If it had a texture, what would it be?
4. If it had a color, what would it look like?
5. Draw a picture of the critic.
6. If it had a name, what would you call it?

How about the highest self? We can invite the same process.

1. How does the highest self feel?
2. What message does it have for me?
3. If it had a texture, what would it be?
4. If it had a color, what would it look like?
5. Draw a picture, or symbol, for the highest self.
6. What would you name your highest self?

Once we can help the client identify both, we can engage these two parts of self in ways that serve the client.

THE INNER DICHOTOMY

As a kid I recalled watching Saturday morning cartoons with Mickey Mouse, Goofy and Donald Duck. Every now and then the character would be faced with making a decision. On one shoulder, an angel appeared and the other, a devil appeared. Each would make a case for what to do. The angel would make a case for doing right and the devil always made the case for being self-serving.

One of my clients named her highest self "Maria." When she felt stuck I would ask, "What would Maria tell you?" Or we made a joke and replaced WWJD (What would Jesus do?) with WWMD (What Would Maria Do?).

The Sufi tradition teaches that we are each born with an inner jewel, which is the heart and essence of what makes me a unique Laurel from all the other Laurels in the world and you, your unique, gifted self. There has never been and never will be another you again in all of time and space.

While we are still alive, we will live this inner dichotomy. Yet, the more we help our clients get in touch with the higher aspects of themselves and who they really are, the more peace and empowerment they live in. While the inner-critic, or ego, never goes away, its voice does diminish the less we invest in it.

Have your clients consider: What is their inner jewel? What name embodies the essence of who they are?

I had the honor of working with Melanie Dewberry. Melanie wrote *The Power of Naming* and developed a naming process based on Native American traditions. After spending a few sessions with you, she intuits a name that is native to you and symbolizes the essence of who you are and your purpose here.

Native Americans have known the power of naming for centuries and named based on the sacred aspects of who someone is, their primary gift, and also called their medicine.

My spiritual native name was given to me by Melanie by working with her through her process. Melanie named me, She Who Roots Us. When she said my name, my heart lit up. It captured the essence of my life purpose and intention.

As you read this manual, my heart smiles each time a lesson helps you root further into your own mastery as a coach and beyond.

Next, we will look at the role of Personal Power and how to help clients live aligned.

ALIGNING PERSONAL POWER

One day I realized, "Oh, gosh. I'm not twenty anymore." I was making so many mistakes at work and not catching them before they impacted other people. It was getting to be very embarrassing. Not only that, but the universe seems to have a principle of patterns. So, the errors would end up impacting the same person often. Each time this was brought to my attention, I would cringe over and over again. I began to self-observe. I noticed when I was moving too fast or multitasking, and my brain started missing things. How frustrating that moving fast and working on multiple items in my twenties was no problem and even fun!

I thought I was not trying hard enough. If I focus even harder, I can still be faster and work on multiple things. So, I pushed myself harder.

How was I giving my power away? On the one hand, I was not accepting what is and how that changed. I began pushing against what is. On the other hand, the push energy took me further out of alignment, and guess what? More mistakes were made and balls were dropped, not less. Healthy internal boundaries with the self and the external world allow us to live fully integrated with our values, through our heart and with our truth. Having healthy internal boundaries is what leads us to be our best in the external world.

An internal boundary is a knowledge of where true self is and living integrated with that knowledge. To live integrated in my 40-year-old self, versus my 20-year-old self meant I accepted "what is" and "what was." I created space in my schedule not to push harder, which allowed me to embrace one project at a time. This alignment kept my power intact. I showed up my best, brought positive energy to my work, and got back to delivering excellence.

Our clients often come to us unaware of where their power leaks are. We can help them locate the power leaks so that they can come up with power patches. Our personal power is like a boat. When intact, we sail far and wide. When there is a leak, the boat begins to sink, and it's all hands on deck.

Here is a list of some of the ways we give our power away:
- o Fighting against "what is"
- o Guilt, shame, envy
- o Inauthenticity – camouflaging
- o Lack of discipline
- o Loose boundaries
- o Lust / greediness
- o Not grieving
- o Over-giving / Overdoing
- o Rigidity
- o Seeking worth externally
- o Taking responsibility for another's feelings
- o Unwillingness
- o Victim stories "I can't"

Helping our clients identify where, how, and why they give their power away to other people or other things is the first step. Next, we can invite them to create a power patch. For example, if your client identifies they give their power away by seeking worth externally, you can help them locate their true self-worth. Or if a client identifies they give their power away by people-pleasing, you can invite them to explore what putting themselves first looks like.

ADDRESSING ENERGY & TIME MANAGEMENT
Time management really boils down to energy management.

There are so many things I want to volunteer for, show up to, and people to be with... With a heavy heart, I can't physically do everything I want to, or, others want me to do. Can you relate?

As coaches, we want to believe we are all unlimited! So, where is the line between the unlimited and the limits and boundaries needing our respect? This is a question that clients often grapple with. Let's examine some key distinctions to bring successful time and energy management to life!

We have daily physical limits such as gravity, fast food intake, sleep, overcommitting, time, money, etcetera. Ignoring physical limitation is a risk to our overall health and vitality, negatively impacting other areas of life.

My oldest son Alec always says, "If only I didn't have to sleep mom, I'd get so much more done!" I totally and completely get it. If I could be in five places at once, and still perform daily with excellence, I'd be game!

Yet, there is a side to our potential that is unlimited. The side coaching brings out in us when we are willing. Not physically but internally. Our self-talk. The internal game either launches us to great heights or brings us down, limiting our every move (often without us knowing it). One thought is all it takes to spiral into either direction! Just one.

Consider this spiritual teaching on fatigue, inspiration, and the human spirit:

> "The result of genuine devotion is inspiration, a word which properly understood is the opposite of fatigue. To be fatigued is to be dis-spirited, but to be inspired is to be in the spirit. To be egocentric is to be dis-spirited, but to be self-centered in the right sense is to be inspired or in spirit. The truly inspired are enlightened and cannot abide in darkness." ACIM T-4.in.1:5-8

As always, there is wisdom in the balance of opposites. This is like a tightrope walk across the line of empowerment anytime we honor our external "limits" and surpass internal "limits." Ignoring the first is a vice and the latter a virtue.

Masterful coaching addresses both... the internal and external apex of potential. It all rests on energy management between the mind, the body, and our human spirit. Energy management is related externally to our self-care measures and internally with what we prioritize and what motivates us.

Have you heard the saying, the deeper the roots, the taller the tree? Self-care is the soil that nourishes our roots. As we nourish our roots, we are able to yield more fruits. Emerson said, "The first wealth is health." Self-care is so centric to our long-term success. How we prioritize our self-care, physically and internally, is key to successful energy management.

TIME MANAGEMENT COACHING

Many clients can grapple with effective time management.

Time management coaching is an opportunity for the client to look at their priorities and see if their priorities are showing up, or not. We can help the client identify what they need to say "yes" to so they know what to say "no" to.

We can also flip the inquiry and ask the client to examine: "What do you need to say no to, so that you can say yes to something greater?"

Effective time management protects our priority and affords us enough energy and focus so that we can work smarter, not harder. Managing time means we are living in choice and not by chance.

> *Time management is really about life management.*
> *Life management is really about priorities.*
> *Priorities are really about aligning with what inspires us.*
> *What inspires us is connected to what we value.*
> *Therefore, time management is about placing that which we value first.*

Hyrum Smith, author of *The 10 Natural Laws of Successful Time & Life Management* identifies five laws that align our time and energy with our core values.

These are:

1. "You control your life by controlling your time."
2. "Your governing values are the foundation of personal fulfillment."
3. "When your daily activities reflect your governing values, you experience inner peace."
4. "To reach any significant goal, you must leave your comfort zone."
5. "Daily planning leverages time through increased focus."

First, is your client aware of what their core values are? Self-awareness around core values is imperative to effectively caring for our time and energy. Second, is self-awareness around limitations.

For example, I submitted an essay to the Better Business Bureau of Southern Arizona. They liked my submission and called me last week to speak to it on video. Law #4 came to mind. "To reach any significant goal, you must leave your comfort zone."

I am an introvert. I would be walking into a video setup with new people I have never met, speaking to something on video, and the only directions I had were to "just show up and read the teleprompter – we picked phrases from your essay." As an introvert, I'm going to manage my time and energy differently than an extrovert. An extrovert may go out to breakfast with coworkers then show up ready to roll. I had to block off extra downtime before the video shoot so that I could show up strong, inspired to be there, and energized. I also protected my time and energy by turning off my cell phone that entire morning and did not take calls until after I was finished.

The outcome?

I showed up ready to roll! They gave me such outstanding feedback. I walked away grateful I created my day in alignment with my recipe for success versus showing up frazzled and scattered had I taken calls and had breakfast with my team prior.

Third, we help the client examine their goals and top priorities.

The concept of time and energy management is rooted in the fundamental coaching tenant:

Every human being has their own unique success formula.

Even though my success formula may look vastly different from your success formula, the principles Hyrum speaks to help inform the way. His core message is that if we wish to shock people with our efficiency, we must set aside time to prepare in advance and choose what shows up. Living by default only gets our client so far.

For those clients that rebel against structure, do not fret! You can invite them to plan for unstructured time too. Success formulas are not all or nothing; they flex to the person. The important thing is that you help your client get back in the driver's seat of their success.

Planning approaches to invite your client to consider or to do with your clients include:

Annual planning:
Annual planning is a powerful way to begin with the end in mind. It is about creating a container for priorities to show up. Steven Covey, the author *of The 7 Habits of Highly Effective People*, noted capacity. He teaches that if we focus on more than three big things at once, we become stretched thin, which drains efficiency.

Quarterly planning:
Quarterly planning is excellent for leaders, business owners, and parents. You can sit down and ensure key events or milestones are being included in all other planning efforts.

Weekly planning:

Weekly planning typically happens on a Sunday or first thing Monday morning. This includes a review of the week and making any needed adjustments. We can delineate projects, schedule extra time for clients, include errands, block off down time, and plan self-care time.

Daily planning:

Daily planning looks at the day ahead and ensures everything is doable. This may include organizing time, moving something around that is less critical or scheduling time where the phone is off and email won't be checked until later.

The other thing to consider around daily time and energy management is a lesson we learn from... ducks. Did you know that ducks prune their feathers in order to stay afloat? They apply an oil slick that allows them to float with ease. Without this, the down feathers would soak up the water and become too heavy to float.

Laurie Beth Jones, who wrote *Jesus in Blue Jeans*, speaks to how when we adopt a morning ritual of self-care it sets up our day to help us stay afloat and endure life's curveballs with greater ease and grace. What would set you up for success each day? Meditation? Going for a walk? Prayer? Other? What formula will set you up for a stellar day?

TIME MANAGEMENT TIP:

My mentor Sandy used to say, "And don't forget to make time for "Unk Unks." The unk unks were her term for the "unknown unknowns" in life. They show up mostly when we set a timeline for three weeks and we end up needing nine weeks. Her rule of thumb I found to be very humbling. Whenever I would state a timeline, she would say, "OK, now times that number by three." This is equally true with budgets. Whatever you think something will cost, make room for error.

Although this approach may feel disheartening to those who are ready to attain our goals yesterday, it is a much more accurate way to plan and ensure we clear enough space on the runway for a successful takeoff and landing.

ELEVATING EMOTIONAL INTELLIGENCE
Emotion truly is our energy in motion.

Emotion is a powerful motivator and understanding the role emotions play in our clients is vital. Developing emotional intelligence (EQ) is one of the most important factors to effective leadership, happy relationships, and living a fulfilling, prosperous life.

In Emotional Intelligence 2.0, authors Travis Bradberry and Jean Greaves, share research on the significance of emotional intelligence. They found:

"EQ is so critical to success that it accounts for 58% of performance in all job types. It's the single biggest predictor of performance in the work-place and the strongest driver of leadership and personal excellence."

"90% of high performers are also high in EQ."

"People with high EQs make more money – an average of $29,000 more per year than people with low EQs. The link between EQ and earnings is so direct that every point increase in EQ adds $1,300 to an annual salary."

Below is a list of 20 interpersonal skills that developing a high EQ helps us master:

1. Anger management	8. Flexibility	15. Social skills
2. Assertiveness	9. Humility	16. Stress management
3. Communication	10. Inclusivity	17. Support
4. Decision making	11. Leadership	18. Time management
5. Empathy	12. Problem solving	19. Transition agility
6. Energy management	13. Relatability	20. Trust
7. Equity	14. Self-accountability	

Emotional intelligence is defined as:
"The skill, or natural ability, to accurately perceive, manage and apply reason to the meaning of emotion in ways that enhance self-understanding and an understanding of others." - Mayer & Salovey

Our emotions are how we experience reality....by feeling it. Mayer & Salovey are key researchers in the early field of EQ, identified four main ingredients of emotional intelligence.

These are:

	EQ In Action:
	Accurately perceives emotion in self and others. We can learn how to pick up on distress cues and respond to them. Learning how to perceive accurately is important so we aren't reacting to assumptions.
	Uses emotions to facilitate thinking. We can learn to use emotions as indicators for something deeper. Emotions reflect back to us our core values, beliefs, and priorities.
	Learn how to manage emotions. We can learn how to notice emotional imbalance and manage our experience. Deep breathing, mediation, and activities that release serotonin are all ways we can manage emotion.
	Understand emotional meaning and interpretations. We can learn how to not confuse an emotion with reality. Because I feel fear doesn't mean I'm in actual danger.

Our emotions reflect where our clients are aligned. Are they living aligned with their inner- critic? Are they living aligned with their highest self? As they answer our questions, they can feel if an answer is in alignment or out of alignment.

We all have an inner compass. We feel our answers. Whether we trust our inner compass or not is another question. In masterful coaching, we invite our clients to trust their inner compass.

Modern culture has created stories and myths around emotions and the role they play.

- emotions are a sign of weakness
- emotions don't belong in the workplace
- emotions are irrational and inhibit us
- emotions leave us out of control
- emotions are worthless
- only good feelings are OK
- emotions are complicated
- emotions happen for no reason
- emotions are un-masculine

We are even taught that love hurts. Yet, love does not hurt. It is the absence of love that hurts.

Helping clients accurately interpret emotions helps them step out of confusion and self- deception. Helping clients use emotions to generate new thinking is an asset to them personally and professionally. Helping clients develop new ways to manage their emotions gives them an advantage.

In essence, helping our clients embrace their emotional capacity elevates their entire life experience. It also helps clients navigate life's rough patches.

"Research showed that leaders
who focus on self-management and relations
produced 390% more."- Goleman, Boyatzis & McKee

Up next, we will explore ways to help support your clients through rough patches.

NAVIGATING ROUGH PATCHES

It may be easy to assume that coaching doesn't address life's rough patches because coaches do not do therapy, give advice, or counsel. This is not so. There is a distinction between a situational issue and a chronic clinical issue. Coaches help with situational rough patches. Therapists are licensed to help aid chronic clinical issues.

As we've explored, in order to move from probability to possibility and attain life's callings, a client must dispel inner obstacles. These can include needing to forgive, needing to grieve, or enduring a dark night of the soul.

In coaching through rough patches, we must also be well aware of our professional scope and may decide to refer out if the client is unable to hold the coaching. If a rough patch turns into a bigger grip on the client that is too big for the client to face in coaching, it is time to refer out.

Below are ways we can help our clients through life's rough patches so that they can continue on their journey to integration.

IMMEDIATE CONCERNS

Imagine this. Your client is buzzing along, six months into their coaching program, making progress and thriving. One day they show up to the session. You ask, "What are we working on today?" They burst out in tears and proceed to inform you their spouse moved out while they were on a work travel trip.

All of a sudden, your thriving client dives into immediate concerns. What do with the house? How to pay the bills? How to understand what and why this just happened? What to do with work? Etcetera.

This is what we call immediate concerns.

It is imperative to note that a client in immediate concerns is not coachable. My mentor Sandy called the state of immediate concerns "Mach 3 hair on fire." If a client is in immediate concerns, we put the coaching aside and instead offer support. They need immediate assistance in getting resources and answering questions. Clients can dive into an immediate concern if there is a job loss, a death in the family, a negative medical diagnosis, or any event that puts them in an immediate need for help.

To help a client get resourced we may:
- Listen with an empathetic ear
- Help them locate resources online
- Sit with them as they make phone calls
- Invite them to list out their entire support system
- Help them figure out their next steps

At this point, the coaching may or may not continue. It is not uncommon to put coaching on hold and resume when things stabilize.

NOTE: If a potential client comes to you for help during a new immediate concern, proceed with caution. They may not be able to hold the coaching and may need resources.
Coaching works best when the client has space to hold the coaching.

To summarize, if a current client ends up in an immediate concern, set aside coaching and offer your assistance to help them get resourced. If a potential client comes to you in immediate concerns, see if they need something else and proceed with caution.

FORGIVENESS

Forgiveness is a hot topic and often wrought with more questions than solid answers. For example, if I forgive, am I approving of what happened? If I forgive am I overlooking? How can I feel angry and still forgive? The problem with forgiveness is that our clients may be afraid of what is on the other side of forgiveness. It is human nature to stay anchored in the upset when we do not forgive.

A Course in Miracles offers a powerful perspective on forgiveness. It teaches that the heart of forgiveness is the recognition that the only thing that ever needs to be forgiven are illusions. Illusions lead to transgressions. People cause damage when living under immense stress and do not know there is a better way. People cause damage when they are reacting to trauma and hurting on the inside. The course teaches that all forms of attack are actually calls for help beneath the surface. What is possible for your client if illusions are the only thing to forgive?

If a client is stuck in a resentment, we can also help them examine their entire relationship to forgivingness. How do they define it? How hard is it to forgive? What does forgiveness look like for them? What other definitions could help? What illusions were at play in creating the hurt?

There is a saying: Hurting people hurt people. What does this tell us about forgiveness? The opposite can also be true. What about those people that hurt us that had good intentions but still caused harm? Forgiveness is also best addressed in the heart. Sometimes people don't forgive to try to protect their hearts. Helping your clients access their heart can help them dispel illusions that keep them stuck in fear of forgiving someone they were hurt by.

These are all avenues for exploration if a client is experiencing resistance or resentments due to a hurting relationship.

GRIEF

One of the ways we may see our clients give their power away is by avoiding grief. Whether they wish to avoid the pain of grief, or just allow life's hustle and bustle to take over, not grieving builds up like plaque in the human heart.

Helping a client explore their definition of and relationship to grief can bring them closer to their truth and help them locate ways they can meaningfully heal from a loss. With issues of grief, it is best to keep empathy near. A client may just need to be heard and share their story of loss. A client may need to spend a few sessions just receiving empathy. That is OK. All loss reminds us that life in the world of relativity is temporary, which can bring up many emotions. Loss can also fuel us to look at and get clear about our values, our bucket list, and our priorities.

When a client is ready and on the other side of the loss, we can offer an invitation to examine what the loss reflected to them about what they cherish most in life. Remember, it is best to refer out if the loss becomes bigger than the client can handle. This is apparent when holding space and empathy alone is not enough or if a loss leads to dark thoughts or suicide ideation.

If the space held through a loss with empathy is enough, then staying put for a session or two can be normal, depending on the situation.

DARK NIGHT OF THE SOUL

A dark night of the soul sounds and feels scarier than it is. In her book "In My Own Words", Mother Theresa spoke of going through dark nights of the soul where she felt distant from God's guidance. She talks of her experience of connection to God came more in ebbs and flows.

Eckhart Tolle defines the dark night of the soul this way:

"It is a term used to describe what one could call a collapse of a perceived meaning in life...an eruption into your life of a deep sense of meaninglessness. The inner state in some cases is very close to what is conventionally called depression. Nothing makes sense anymore, there's no purpose to anything. Sometimes it's triggered by some external event, some disaster perhaps, on an external level. The death of someone close to you could trigger it, especially premature death, for example if your child dies. Or you had built up your life, and given it meaning – and the meaning that you had given your life, your activities, your achievements, where you are going, what is considered important, and the meaning that you had given your life for some reason collapses." (8)

On a positive note, the dark night can be an existential breakdown that can lead to a greater breakthrough. There is no light when a caterpillar goes into a chrysalis, and the metamorphosis process is quite unbelievable. The caterpillar's body somehow magically transforms into an entirely different body with a full set of legs, fully developed, patterned wings, a new capacity to fly, an adult reproductive system, and a brand-new set of antennae.

The caterpillar transforms when it reaches its full capacity as a caterpillar.

How does the caterpillar rearrange itself into a butterfly? It releases an enzyme that dissolves its tissue. The scientists call this "caterpillar soup." It has cells that are ready to become each body part that survive the dissolving process. These cells are called "imaginal discs." These cells then use the "soup" to grow the blueprint of the butterfly. (10)

Are we not the same, spiritually speaking?

When we reach our full capacity, do we sink into profound questions (cocoon). As we realize what served us in the past is not what we want for our future (dissolving) and we imagine a new purpose or direction (imaginal disc begins to shape the future) and we decide to change course and expand our life (come of out of the cocoon and take flight).

Eckhart Tolle continues:

"[People] awaken into something deeper, which is no longer based on concepts in your mind. A deeper sense of purpose or connectedness with a greater life that is not dependent on explanations or anything conceptual any longer. It's a kind of re-birth. The dark night of the soul is a kind of death that you die. What dies is the egoic sense of self. Of course, death is always painful, but nothing real has actually died there – only an illusory identity. Now it is probably the case that some people who've gone through this transformation realized that they had to go through that in order to bring about a spiritual awakening. Often it is part of the awakening process, the death of the old self and the birth of the true self." (8)

If your client is going through a dark night of the soul, it may appear that they are going backwards in their progress, when in fact they may be repositioning all they thought was real and facing their inner world to help shape a new future.

This can be a powerful and potentiated time for coaching.

How do you want to support your client going through such a transformation? How comfortable can you be sitting in the uncomfortable with your client? How can you see the butterfly while the client is just starting to spin the cocoon?

I endured a dark night of the soul while going through a divorce. My coach and mentor Sandy right out asked me if I was in the dark night of the soul. I realized I was. I was questioning what I valued and wanted out of life, I grappled with regrets and confusions, and I was getting clear about what I didn't want. This isn't easy work, but it is deeply transformational.

Tips for helping a client through the dark night:
1. Keep it simple. Invite the client to pick one topic to focus on a time. A dark night often has us swimming in myriad emotions, thoughts, and fears. Focusing on one at a time will help.
2. Invite learning. Questions around self-awareness, like, "What are you learning about yourself?" and "How can what you learn to show up in other areas of your life?" invite the integration process to continue so that the client doesn't get caught too long in the cocoon.
3. Be empathetic. "Of course. It makes sense to me that you feel sadness." Relating can help the client feel safe and heard so that coming out of the cocoon looks and feels more appealing than staying stuck.
4. Remember, "This too shall pass." A rough patch is just a season. The butterfly is on the other side. Holding this space is you believing in the client when they can't yet believe in themselves.

It is also worth noting that some clients disappear during this time. It is not personal. As the coach, it is best practice to check on them if you have permission to do so. It is important your client knows you care about them.

It can also help to have some resources or literature to recommend or send. There are books and articles written on the dark night. Depending on your niche, you may wish to find one that fits your clientele.

Remember, the night is always the darkest right before dawn.

VISITING THE BIG PICTURE

At least once in every session, I love to take a bird's-eye view. A bird's-eye view reminds the client of the bigger picture of their life. It includes future goals, guiding values, top priorities, and broader perspectives. The bigger picture is just that... bigger. It contains a wider variety of solutions and perspectives.

Visiting the bigger picture helps the client be forward-moving and forward-thinking while going through a rough patch. It can also help them get out of the weeds of an issue and back into choice. When we see a bigger picture, we can see the whole of something and put things in perspective.

I was backcountry adventure hiking once (no trail) and made it to the top of a huge hill. Before descending to a canyon below, I took in the lay of the land. I could see the canyon we were heading towards and the fork of the canyon creek. The fork meant there were options. Take the creek east or take it west, or follow it south.

When the big picture is clear,
options appear.

How do we take our clients into a bigger picture? Through our questions that invite bigger perspectives.

Consider some of these:

- *Ten years from now, will this issue matter?*
- *Who is the wisest person you know? What would they tell you?*
- *Let's say it's ten years from now. What solution would you love to have tried?*
- *If you were on top of a mountain looking at this issue, what would you see differently?*
- *What's the bigger picture here?*
- *What do you need to say no to, to say yes to something greater?*
- *What else?*

CHAPTER SEVEN

ഔ   Coaching to Integrative Awareness   ൙

"The directions of integration and disintegration help us recognize
whether we are progressing or regressing in our development."
"Integration gives us objective markers of our growth.
Disintegration shows us how we act out under stress,
what our unconscious motivations and behaviors are,
and, paradoxically, what qualities we most need to integrate."
~ *The Wisdom of the Enneagram, Riso & Hudson*

Now that we have a path for coaching a client from their wholeness, we can begin to examine integration and growth. Wholeness informs growth.

We will start the exploration by looking at gaining integrative awareness. Then in Chapter Eight, we will look at the skills and frameworks for coaching to integration.

We will start by examining the opposite of integrative awareness and see how that has limitations. It is essential to know the cost and payoffs we face if we wish to break away from limited ways of being and embrace a better way.

After looking at the bigger picture, we will circle back to examine what integrative awareness and integration look like in coaching.

ADVANCING BEYOND LIMITATION

When single-use plastic was invented, it was "genius." We could have something wrapped until we got home and simply toss it out when done using it. Who would have thought it would pile up to an island of waste, the size of Texas, spanning across five oceans and killing sea life?

When Karl Benz invented the first gas-powered car, it was brilliant. (3) No need to walk or hassle with horses as you go from place to place. Who would have thought cars, transportation, and planes would be what they are today? Who would have imagined the daily pollution would pour into the atmosphere faster than we can clean it up? There are places in Mexico City and China where you can't even see the sky and are advised to wear masks because the pollution is so thick.

The Industrial Age created corporatocracies that focused on strict policies to keep people safe and maximize production. At the same time, they navigated an environment full of heavy machinery and assembly lines. For safety, managers adopted a "shut-up and do what I say" approach. Who would have thought those mindsets would remain for decades and cease to be effective, no longer needed, thus limiting managers in their greatness and leadership capacities. (5)

When I was a young girl frolicking in the country and climbing apple trees, I never imagined 40 years later having to contend with five out of seven family members being on their cell phones at a holiday gathering. Or cancer going from a rarity to a very heart-wrenching normality.

What do all of these modern day events have in common? They all stem from linear approaches.

I am taking a strong stand that the time for linear approaches has run its course; linear processes are inherently limited, yielding greater consequences than solutions. I invite you to consider an Integratively intelligent approach instead.

We are at the moment in humanity where small things like throwing away dried-up Sharpies, mounds of junk mail, and tossing Christmas packaging in the trash has added up to big things. We are facing large-scale impact never before seen and never before foreseen.

Linear solutions = Limited outcomes

Although we are facing large-scale ramifications of linear approaches, they do have their place. As my mentor, Sandy Hogan, put it, "Different times, different things." Below is a taxonomy of the pros and cons of linear thinking.

PROs	CONs
<ul><li>Fits a simple standard format. Ex: single-focused business proposals.</li><li>Simplistic logic.</li><li>Provides quick solutions.</li><li>Streamlines outcomes.</li><li>Provides laser focus.</li><li>Accomplishes single goals.</li></ul>	<ul><li>Excludes the big picture.</li><li>Leads to blinders and biases.</li><li>Keeps us "in the box."</li><li>Short-sighted decision-making.</li><li>Doesn't ask "why", preventing better solutions.</li><li>Capacities go untapped.</li><li>Opposes nature by compartmentalizing.</li><li>Allopathic (linear) medical approaches treat or repress symptoms without healing the cause.</li></ul>

Sandy also shared, "As you can see, there is room for both. The wisdom is when, where, and why both linear and integrative have a place." As we move forward as a human race, there is wisdom in knowing when an asset becomes a liability.

In a 2019 interview with Sandy, she proceeded to share with me that if you see a brain surgeon, you need them to be single-focused on extracting the tumor without causing harm first.

So, yes, there is a time for linear thinking. Getting short-term laser-focused results, for example. Yet, to remain in linear thinking mode when it comes to larger impact is like placing blinders on.

Is success a true success if there is a negative consequence on the other end? I say no. Whether we want to acknowledge it or not, all things in life are interconnected. To impact one part impacts other parts. There is no way around this. This is a law of cause and effect.

So, what is on the other side? If not linear thinking, then what?

What if we include all aspects? What if we see cause/effect as a positive awareness? What if we release the blinders of bias?

Then we have the birthplace of Integrative Intelligence.

Whether or not we acknowledge it, interdependence and interconnectivity are the very fabric of all physical reality and all of humanity.

> *Interconnectivity makes up the very fabric*
> *of all physical reality and all of humanity.*

Furthermore, as we begin to view life through its interconnectivity, we naturally yield the most impressive insights and more effective results. Realizing and embracing interconnectivity, interrelatedness, and interdependency is the heart, blood, and bones of Integrative Intelligence.

Employing Integrative Intelligence maximizes intended consequences by minimizing unintended consequences. Humanity is now dealing with margins of error that carry negative implications, and this need not be.

With integrative thinking, we upgrade the "win" model, graduate to the "win-win" model, and begin to expand even further into a "win-win-win-win" model. In other words, not only is a company successful financially ("win"), but the environment benefits from the products/services("win"), the employees benefit("win"), the CEO benefits("win"), and the customers benefit("win"). Versus the old linear approach: the company is financially successful (win), and the CEO benefits (win). Employees, the environment, and customers do not benefit fully (lose-lose-lose).

Consequences of Integrative Intelligence:
- Win-win-win-win: The individual (the "I"), the larger community of people involved (the "We"), the movement created (the "It"), and the environment (the "Its).
- Zero to little adverse side effects.
- Maximizes intended consequences, minimizes unintended consequences.
- No settling for "tradeoffs" or singular successes.
- Collaboration takes priority over linear competition.
- People are prioritized over profit, ironically leading to greater profit. (1)

Why produce tradeoffs when we can invite our full potential to come forward? Are we too unintelligent to operate without causing large scale harm?

The answer is…no. We are not an unintelligent species. Far from it. But, we are a biased species. Linear thinking creates bias, conscious or unconscious. Biases place limits, visible or not. Intended, or not. Biases put us in the box.

Can you imagine if cars were zero emissions from the beginning? Can you imagine seeing the sky in Mexico City on a clear day? Can you imagine no plastic cluttering up the land and oceans? Imagine garbage that decomposes? There would be no landfills full of billions of pounds of grotesque trash mounds that we pretend do not exist and are growing daily.

Is this possible? Yes. Is this plausible? Is this plausible? Not until we welcome our full capacity. Not until we start to act from the wisdom of interconnectivity. Not until we embrace our ability for Integrative Intelligence.

There is good news, though! Large-scale impact goes in many directions. One change to a large-scale corporation completely changes the outcome. If one area producing 500 tons of pollution shifts to sustainable ways, they just eliminated a future of exponential pollution in that area and all the areas that are impacted.

THE ONUS

Who is responsible? Is it the government, the people, the company leaders, stakeholders, board members, individuals, groups?

No matter what the subject, whether it is politics, environment, ethics, or living, the answer remains the same. The onus is at the feet of cause first and effect second. I am responsible for what I cause. I am responsible for my choices. Anything I choose that yields an outcome and carries an impact, I am responsible for overseeing. I am responsible for any area I have impact over and for my impact on any other areas impacted secondarily.

I can ignore my responsibility, but the onus still falls at the level of causation.

First onus: Person or group creating impact (can choose differently) Second onus: Anyone supporting the impact (can speak up)
Third onus: The impacted (can set a boundary)

We see companies deflect the onus, and people negatively impacted are up speaking up. If we are operating integratively and intelligently, we would not need to settle for "solutions" or products or anything that caused damage or had a negative impact attached to it.

You can't tell me we are not intelligent enough to not settle for short-sighted and harmful outcomes. It is time we wake up to our full human potential and stop settling.

RE-IMAGINE

Imagine reading a story to your grandchild decades from now, laughing at how ridiculous our silly ways used to be.

It makes sense the inventors of the past stopped after they reached their single goal. We had no clue what large-scale impact was back then. Now, we know better. We can do better.

Will we?

This is where coaches step in. Coaches are helping us do better. Coaches are raising the bar on success. Coaches are the pioneers for a better way and help companies, leaders, and individuals to shape a profound future.

Up next, we will explore the profound role of coaching in modern-day societies. Summary:
- Integrative Intelligence evokes success in all areas.
- Linear thinking yields limited results.
- Negative large-scale impact is the result of linear thinking.
- Large-scale impact can go in either direction, positive or negative.
- Positive large-scale impact is the result of Integrative Intelligence.

The time for integrative intelligence is here. It is time to pivot into our full potential. Let's explore how we can do this.

CULTIVATING THE DOMAINS OF HUMAN POTENTIAL
in·tel·li·gence
/in'teləjəns/

"The ability to acquire and apply knowledge and skills." Oxford

We are multidimensional beings that often end up ensnared by one or two main domains, unaware of how each impacts the others. To cultivate all domains of human potential is the heart of understanding Integrative Intelligence.

Human potential and the capacity for developing intelligence are intimately interwoven. We reach new potential as we develop our intelligence, integrate these intelligences, and reach new levels of capacity as new possibilities are unlocked.

Now let's take a closer look at each domain.

The 8 Domains:
1. Somatic
2. Cognitive
3. Emotional
4. Energetic
5. Relational
6. Motivational
7. Spiritual
8. Integrational

Understanding each domain helps inform our coaching as we invite our clients to move into alignment and develop a fuller capacity. One of the ways is to recognize the interconnected nature of the domains. For example, by developing my awareness of my motivations in life, I empower my capacity for healthy relationships in the relational domain. Developing my spiritual capacity may positively impact my emotional and cognitive life.

Inquiring into what domains support other domains can be a powerful consideration for clients to examine. If the client is struggling in one domain, what other domains can be engaged to help?

Another powerful way to engage the 8 Domains in coaching is by examining where our alignment is found. We can invite our clients to consider and identify how they get out of balance in each domain. We can invite our clients to consider how they "over-do" or "under-do." As growing and evolving human beings, balance and alignment is one way we sustain long-term success.

Each of these domains are also ways we can experience balance and imbalance in life. In this regard, we help our clients maximize their potential by cultivating balance in each area.

Questions to give our clients:
- ✓ How aware am I of each domain of my potential?
- ✓ How often do I consider each domain when making a decision?
- ✓ Am I cultivating healthy and sustainable growth in each domain?
- ✓ How aware am I of being in balance and out of balance in each domain?

As clients complete their coaching program, we can invite them to self-examine growth in each domain. This self-assessment spotlights their next growth phase and is how we can graduate the client.

"In this regard, the client continues to become skillful in the absence of the coach."
~ Sandy Hogan

Somatic Domain: The Body

The body is our vessel for life, energy, and action. Emerson is quoted as saying, "The first wealth is health." When we have health, we are free to explore life uninhibited. "The problem is that some of us become uninhabited," said Sandy Hogan. When we forget to inhabit our bodies, we ignore critical feedback mechanisms.

Balance in this domain entails cultivating healthy habits, understanding the body's cues, respect for the body's needs, limitations, and cultivating a healthy body image.

The body offers a gateway into self-awareness. It issues cues to unconscious beliefs, wounds, and unmet needs. These cues also alert us to self-deception.

Coaching Questions:
1. In what ways do you care, respect, or disparage the body?
2. What is your relationship to your body?
3. Can you see your body as sacred?
4. What feedback have you ignored?
5. What are your addictions?
6. Ways you over-do?
7. Ways you under-do?
8. What does balance look like for you in this domain?

Key qualities of mastery:
- ✓ Understanding the body's feedback mechanisms
- ✓ Responding to and honoring physical limitation
- ✓ Responding to and honoring physical needs
- ✓ Engaging the body to support mind, emotion and energy
- ✓ Revering the body as a sacred vessel to care for
- ✓ Revering the body as temporary
- ✓ Cultivating physical energy

Cognitive Domain: Mind Over Matter

The mind is a powerful tool for understanding contrast, creating distinctions, forming beliefs, and inhabiting habits. The mind allows us to soak up new learning and expand our knowledge base. Through the mind, we reason and communicate.

In this domain, we "catch ourselves in the act" through mental perception and have the ability to make adjustments that create new potentials for ourselves and others.

Balance in this domain includes self-reflection, self-awareness, and moving from a fixed mindset to a growth mindset.

Coaching Questions:

1. How can you unlearn that which no longer serves you?
2. How do you learn new things after unlearning?
3. Are you aware of your fixed mindsets?
4. Do you embody a growth mindset?
5. How do you locate missing information?
6. Ways you over-do?
7. Ways you under-do?
8. What does balance look like for you in this domain?

Key qualities of mastery:
- ✓ Understanding truth
- ✓ Recognizing illusions
- ✓ Cultivating an inner neutral witness
- ✓ Willingness to face the real
- ✓ Living self-aware
- ✓ Placing the mind in allegiance to the heart
- ✓ Understanding truth is simple

Emotional Domain: Experience

This domain is pertinent if we are to discern and understand our emotional states and what they have to reflect about our levels of self-understanding.

Emotional literacy is elementary in understanding ourselves, relating more deeply to others, cultivating a broader range of human respect, and gaining deeper insights into the plight of the human experience as a whole.

Balance in this domain includes cultivating emotional perception, healthy emotional management, and understanding emotional value.

Coaching Questions:

1. Can you see the message behind the emotions?
2. How can you process strong emotions?

3. Do you embrace emotional experiences or judge them?

4. Do you have emotional addictions?

5. Ways you over-do?

6. Ways you under-do?

7. What does balance look like for you in this domain?

Key qualities of mastery:
- ✓ Perceiving emotions accurately
- ✓ Using emotions to facilitate new thought
- ✓ Managing emotional responses
- ✓ Understanding emotional meaning
- ✓ Receiving and giving love through hardship
- ✓ Engaging the fun aspects of life and laughter
- ✓ Listening to and trusting our emotional inner-compass
- ✓ Being emotionally available

Energetic Domain: Attitude = Outcome

"Everything is energy and that is all there is to it. Match the frequency of the reality you want and you cannot help but get that reality. It can be no other way. This is not philosophy. This is physics." – Einstein

Where our focus is, there is our energy investment. If we focus on our anger for too long, we will project anger and may incite it in others.

Where we invest our energy determines our outcomes. The energy we put out reflects what comes back to us. How can we guard our energy, keep our energy purely intentioned, and use our energy for good?

Energy is one out of our four key resources; time, energy, talent, money.

Balance in this domain includes awareness, cultivation, intentional shifting, and choosing the energy we want to put into our life.

Coaching Questions:
1. How aware are you of your energy and others?
2. Are you aware of the energy you project out?
3. Do you cultivate your energy?
4. How grounded is your energy grounded?
5. How do you put positive energy into a challenge?
6. What can you do to re-set your energy?
7. Ways you over-do?
8. Ways you under-do?
9. What does balance look like for you in this domain?

Key qualities of mastery:
- ✓ Understanding each human virtue carries its own energy
- ✓ Choosing what energy we wish to engage
- ✓ Choosing what we wish to be the possibility of
- ✓ Moving energy through the body so it doesn't stagnate
- ✓ Reads energy without interpretation

Relational Domain: Relationship to Self and Others

As human beings, we do not live alone. We live in community and are connected to our human race as a whole. We have the option of cultivating, initiating, and sustaining heartfelt, intimate connections. There are four primary relationships we form, consciously or unconsciously. These are relationships with ourselves, with others, to what is, and to what is not.

The relationships we form within these four areas can maximize our life experience or drain us. Balance in this domain includes the ability to foster and sustain long-term healthy relationships in all four quadrants. Forming a positive relationship to self is imperative to our health. Developing meaningful, caring, long-term relationships with others helps us live rich, safe, and fulfilled lives. Forming healthy responses to what is and to what isn't allows us to navigate life with mastery.

Coaching Questions:

1. How is your relationship to self?
2. Are you able to self-advocate?
3. Are you aware of how you relate to others?
4. How do you care for your long-term relationships?
5. Do you respectfully relate to those you do not align with?
6. Can you cultivate a bigger picture?
7. What is your relationship to what is not?
8. Ways you over-do?
9. Ways you under-do?
10. What does balance look like for you in this domain?

Key qualities of mastery:
- ✓ Understanding our self-worth
- ✓ Carries clean motivations when relating
- ✓ Chooses our relational responses
- ✓ Understanding our impact on others
- ✓ Intentionally relates through the true-self
- ✓ Dispels "boxes" of judgment
- ✓ Relates through the heart

Motivational Domain: Motive, Intent, Legacy & Calling

In this domain, we explore our life's why, our deeper motivations, passions, purpose, and legacy. We look at how we show up personally and professionally and the ways in which we contribute to our world of relationships. When in balance, this domain includes an understanding of our motivations, intentions, and motivators. This awareness allows us to utilize our strengths, gifts, and passions towards a purpose or as a way to give back and contribute.

Coaching Questions:

1. Are you aware of your motives?
2. What motivates you and inspires you?
3. Are you in touch with your contributions?

4. Are you aligned with your life's callings?

5. What legacy is there for you to leave?

6. Are you aligned with your passions and purpose?

7. Ways you over-do?

8. Ways you under-do?

9. What does balance look like for you in this domain?

Key qualities of mastery:
- ✓ Connects through inspiration
- ✓ Understands underlying motivations
- ✓ Chooses motivations
- ✓ Seeks purpose and intention in actions
- ✓ Acts in service of or to
- ✓ Engages purpose and meaning in life

Spiritual Domain: Connecting to the Web of Life

Our spiritual life is our connection to that which is greater than ourselves. It is developing meaning beyond the self alone. Through this connection to something greater, we connect to a fuller version of life and move beyond the ego. Spirituality may or may not include religious beliefs and take the form of deeper meaning. In our youth, this may be awe at nature, and in our elder years, this may mean volunteering at the local library.

Balance in this domain includes connecting to that which is greater than the egoic self. Questions:
1. What does spirituality mean to you?

2. How big of a picture can you connect with?

3. What takes your breath away?

4. What is your inner "Yes" that lights you up?

5. Ways you over-do?

6. Ways you under-do?

7. What does balance look like for you in this domain?

Key qualities of mastery:

- ✓ Develops a personal definition of spirituality
- ✓ Cares more about attuning than attaining
- ✓ Invests resources beyond the self through contribution
- ✓ Listens for, and follows callings
- ✓ Maintains a spiritual practice in support of all other domains
- ✓ Embodies the spiritual element of life

Integrating Domain: Living Fully

The more we integrate, the more we step into, the higher aspects of self. In this domain, we see integratively, act integratively, and embrace the fullest version of self. Integration allows us to face anything masterfully, allowing our personal power to come from within. In this domain, all is embraced. We see beyond the material. We see above. We see below. We see the history of the past. We see a vision for the future.

Balance in this domain includes seeing and approaching all of life through its interconnectivity and cultivating our Integrative Intelligence.

Coaching Questions:
1. What do you avoid examining within your life?
2. Where are you incongruent? Where do you hide?
3. Where are you single-focused?
4. How can you move towards integration?
5. Ways you over-do?
6. Ways you under-do?
7. What does balance look like for you in this domain?

Key qualities of mastery:

- ✓ Faces all aspects
- ✓ Seeks the win-win-win-win
- ✓ Embraces the fullest frame of life
- ✓ Self-aware, self-generating and sustains success
- ✓ Moves up the level of integration

THE LEVELS OF INTEGRATION

As we grow in our human capacity, we move up the levels of integration. There are three states we can embody on the path to integration:
- Integrated
- Non-Integrated
- Disintegrated

The lower levels are often referred to as "Disintegrated," "Unhealthy," or "Pathological."

Despite brain intelligence, there are low to no levels of self-awareness, self-reflection, or responsiveness in a state of disintegration.

Disintegration is caused by extreme stress or trauma. High levels of reactivity and impulsiveness characterize this state.

Disintegration and pathology is the state of being that supports behaviors such as sex trafficking, drug addiction, bullying, mass shootings, racism, identify theft, and much more. Mismanagement, domestic violence, hacking, gang violence, and organized crime all subside here. A state of disintegration is the common denominator.

The next state is non-integrated. This state is characterized by new self-awareness. At this stage, the capacity to learn and develop becomes available. We can discover our core values, access our innate gifts, and self-reflect. Most people will hang out here unless they experience extreme stress and disintegrate or make the personal choice to integrate.

The third state is called "Healthy" or "Integrated." This state is where we can experience our wholeness and our fullest capacity. In the state of integration, we return to choice, become big picture problem solvers, and cultivate integrative intelligence by considering the integrated nature of all things.

Don Riso and Russ Hudson, the founders of the Enneagram Institute, have studied the levels of development extensively and located nine levels we move up as we integrate into our full potential.

	Levels of Development Outlined by The Enneagram Institute
Healthy	1. Liberation 2. Psychological Capacity 3. Social Value
Average	4. Imbalance / Social Role 5. Interpersonal Control 6. Overcompensation
Unhealthy	7. Violation 8. Obsession and Compulsion 9. Pathological Destructiveness

https://www.enneagraminstitute.com/how-the-enneagram-system-works

- How do we end up at a level?
- How do up-level?
- What causes lower levels to resurface?

In a nutshell, the theory I've landed on through my research and study of the Enneagram systems is that we are born whole. We grow and default to average levels unless something invites us to elevate or pushes us down into unhealthy ranges. For example, if we endure trauma or significant wounding, we establish defense mechanisms to stay safe and disintegrate under stress. On the other hand, if we have a mentor or community that invites us to live through our wholeness, then we experience integration.

In a class taught by Riso and Hudson, I learned that there is a level that we typically hang out at. If we choose to explore our potential, we begin to move up the ladder of integration. As we integrate, we move up to the next level.

Under stress, we move down 1-2 levels. After the stressor passes, we go back to our normal level. As we integrate, we go back down the levels less and less.

Example A: Stress

Let's say my normal stage of integration is "Non-Integrated." Within this stage, let's say I'm at level 5, "Interpersonal Control." Then let's say a stressful event happens, like a minor car accident. Under stress, I go down two levels to level 7, "Violation." Returning to old defense mechanisms is a normal stress reaction.

Example B: Personal Development

I normally live at level 5, "Interpersonal Control," and I have space and support to begin self- developing. In that case, I will change my normative way of being and move up to level 4 capacity, "Social Role."

Example C: Trauma

I normally live at level 5, "Interpersonal Control," and experience trauma like domestic violence. In that case, I am at risk of moving into a complete state of disintegration to self- protect. Trauma puts us in a state of emotional emergency, and our defense mechanisms can become fully engaged.

INCREASING CAPACITY

It is best to look at integration as an increased capacity. What does this mean exactly? Recall the story I shared around choice versus reaction? It went like this: In a coaching session with my mentor Sandy, I said, "I can't believe I made so many dumb choices." She said, "Did you choose?" I said, "Well, yes. Nobody else made those choices but me." She said, "Did you choose? Or did you react?"

This is a powerful distinction. When we react, we are not in choice.

> *"No one decides against his happiness,*
> *but he may do so if he does not see he does it."*
> *- A Course In Miracles*

Let's unpack the stages in greater details:

INTEGRATED	– Resourced – Lives at cause: responsive disposition – Full self-awareness – Self-regulation – Growth mindset, unbiased – Virtuous internally and externally – Solution orientation	– Positive contribution – Big picture problem solver – Lives through gifts – Lives with purpose and meaning – Rises above stressors
NON-INTE-GRATED	– Resourced – Teeters between cause and effect – Situational self-awareness – Situational self-regulation – Teeters between growth and fixed/bias mindset – Teeters between solutions and defense mechanisms	– Capacity expands – Self-agency is gained

DISINTE-GRATED	– Extreme struggle to survive
	– Not resourced
	– Lives at effect: reactive
	– Lack of self-awareness
	– Self-sabotage
	– Fixed mindset, bias fixation
	– Violent: internally or externally
	– Victim orientation
	– Lives through defenses
	– Pathological
		– Anxiety
		– Depression
		– Reacting against self and others:
		  o Addiction
		  o Domestic & public violence
		  o Looting
		  o Sex trafficking
		  o Suicide / Homicide
		  o Theft / Hacking
		  o Unethical policies

The Levels of Integration are a powerful tool to help our clients see the path ahead and realize expansion is possible. Integrative coaching provides excellent shortcuts towards our potentials.

Thinking big-picture, we can see how these levels impact our communities. If we want to see the lower-level issues minimized and live in a safer, emotionally balanced, society then it is time we awaken to our fuller potential and provide more avenues to integration.

The US forefathers said it the best, "United We Stand. Divided We Fall." It is time to embrace our humanity and create space for people to develop their talents, move into their hearts and reach their potentials.

REALIZING THE BOX DOESN'T EXIST

The Arbinger Institute identified four primary self-deception boxes we put ourselves in when we stop relating to others through our hearts and instead live inside of fear. These boxes fragment us off and limit us. These are:

1. "I am better than…."
2. "I am less than…."
3. "I deserve…"
4. "I must be seen as…"

These are the ego's best friends. The ego lives through the separate "I." The ego's version of "I am" is judgmental and separates us from our true self and from others.

Our essence lives with the embrace of "I Am." The "I" sees itself as separate, alone, and independent. The "I Am" understands all of the virtues of self and sees the self integratively connected to all that is. The "I Am" part of us has no need for judgments of good, bad, right, or wrong. "I Am" includes all the qualities that make us human. As I declare "I Am courageous" I activate the possibility of courage within.

Our essence lives with the embrace of "I Am." The "I" sees itself as separate, alone, and independent. The "I Am" understands the virtues of self and sees the self integratively connected to all that is. The "I Am" part of us does not need good, bad, right, or wrong judgments. "I Am" includes all the qualities that make us human. As I declare, "I Am courageous," I activate the possibility of courage within.

The egoic self only lives through fabricated fantasy and reacts as if separate from others. The essence of who we are lives through choice and is aware of interconnectivity. The wisdom of understanding our interconnected nature places us at the cause of our life. While the ego lives in reaction, placing us at the effect in our life.

When we are born into the world, into a body, and we develop a mind, we unilaterally develop defense mechanisms to keep us safe when we realize we can feel pain. Our first wounding sets into action brilliantly manufactured ego beliefs to prevent further harm. In youth, this serves us well. The problem? In adulthood, those brilliantly manufactured defenses, beliefs, and mechanisms are the very constructs that keep us boxed in and limited as we step out of victim (defendant) and into warrior (independent). They become our biggest illusions.

Living through our defenses as we realize our independence keeps us pushing against life and locked into patterned ways of being that do not fully serve our fuller potential. We may become "the good girl" or the "dutiful man" to not rock the boat. We may become a salesperson and learn to sway people so we can stay one step ahead. Or we may strive to be the competent expert or successful person to prove our value or anchor in our "safety" in this crazy, big world. The bigger truth is that safety is an inside job and comes from living in truth and will never be found in an illusion.

Our defenses are not the truth of who we are. When we live through them, we live inside a nicely fabricated box of limitations. When we wonder why we are not happy, not fulfilled, or are waking up feeling an empty hole in our heart, then we are experiencing the ego convincing us we are a separate self. Our authenticity, our true self, our essence, is gently waiting just to be recognized. In reality, we are already whole.

> *"You have taught what you are,*
> *but have not let what you are teach you."*
> *- A Course In Miracles*

AVOIDING MINDSET PITFALLS

The world of illusion can take many forms. Illusions are tricky. They act as unconscious power leaks every time we believe in them or invest our energy in them. Mindset pitfalls are ways we can listen and help our clients locate their fixed mindsets so that you can help your client remove any limitations.

MINDSET PITFALLS:
- Assumptions
- Black/white thinking
- Catastrophizing
- Exaggerating
- Generalizing
- Justifications
- Minimizing
- Self-deprecation
- Specializing
- Pessimism
- Projecting
- Rigidity

While these mindset pitfalls are good to be aware of and can be helpful to identify the ways that we can get in our own way, it is worthy to note that only truth exists. In masterful coaching, we bring our clients back down to reality. Back home to truth, away from the pitfall of illusion and into their true power.

Below are examples of self-awareness exercises:

- Catch yourself in the act of exaggerating and ask yourself what motivated the exaggeration.
- What does it feel like when you begin catastrophizing? How does this inhibit you?
- What are the assumptions you are working from as you move forward? Can you list them out?

Helping your clients catch themselves in the act of any mindset pitfall and become more intentional with their thoughts helps them stay fully aligned with their personal power.

PIVOTING TO OUR TRUTH

There are many ways we can pivot in life. I'm going to share with you my personal experience with the power of pivoting.

I discovered that I kept giving my power away. As a director, I tried so hard to please everyone, yet I wasn't able to. No matter how hard my ego tried to shapeshift "in service" to others, someone was always upset. I took my issue into coaching. Deep down, I was terrified someone would be mad at me for saying no. I discovered that I had been carrying around an underlying false belief for decades. I believed that I was safe only when I adapted to other people's needs.

How did I discover this?

I kept bumping up against negative outcomes. I was horrible at direct communication. If any "negative" feedback needed to be brought up with an employee, I walked on eggshells and tried to skirt around the issue. If the belief that I am only safe when I adapt to others was false. Then what was true? Coaching helped me discover that I am safe when I direct through my heart.

We swim through thousands of thoughts every day. Our thoughts generate many of our emotions. If I perceive I'm unsafe my heart will pound and I'll experience fear. Whether I'm actually unsafe, or not, my body will react to that thought.

Where did the thought come from? My interpretation of what is. The brain is wired for safety. Flight, fight or freeze. The brain, the ego's home, is continually scanning for safety and interpreting what is happening. The problem is when perceiving turns into falsely believing.

We live at the level of thought and emotion quite naturally; however, the beliefs we harbor below, conscious or unconscious, are running the show.

In coaching, if a person's mind is reeling, this indicates a false and limiting belief under the surface. I invite them beneath the surface to the belief running the show. Once they locate the false belief, they connect with what is actually true and then like clockwork... The ego lets go. They become grounded in the new truth. One false impression can send the mind reeling into thousands of doubting, justifying, fearful thoughts. One true belief grounds us into ourselves and generates peace and empowerment.

Back to my example of the false belief that had me reeling. "I am safe if I adapt to other people." I am not sure where I picked this one up along my four decades of life. In belief work, it doesn't always matter. What matters is that we pivot from the false limitation, to the true and possible. In a leadership role as a director, this belief significantly hampered my ability to be a strong leader. When an issue arose, I froze.

The positive side was that belief led me to be a preventer. Because I was not adept at conflict, I became masterful in preventing conflict. Yet, no matter how much prevention one does, conflict will arise. And preventing led to catastrophizing and was exhausting. What did I learn? The ego's illusions always equate to a win-lose formula. When we live through our wholeness, we generate win-win-win formulas.

What was actually true was that I was safest in leadership roles when I chose and stood for a clear direction. This anchored me into being of service to the bigger picture while offering a safe container for conflict to come up. I was able to see "conflicts" as opportunities to get on the same page, or not. Either was OK. As we switch unconscious limiting beliefs into conscious, true beliefs, we expand our capacity to fuel new possibilities.

Limitation only exists in our beliefs. Our beliefs limit or expand our life. I'm sure you have heard, or experienced, how change is hard. If you think about it, change is impossible. What is in the past is in the past. We can't change the past, but we can choose a new possibility. This new choice gives the appearance of change. Can you change what is not come to be? Think about this. The brain's neuropathways are already instilled. Our conditioned ways of being, default reactions are all stored in the brain. The more we use that pathway, the more the brain continues to follow that neuropathway.

So how do we change a neuropathway? We don't have to. It is easier to create a new neuropathway than to focus on changing the old one. The more we focus on the behavior we don't want, the more we are instilling that neuropathway. Instead, we can shift the focus towards the new possibility.

Once I switched from the limit to the truth, my conversations were not founded on eggshells. They were grounded, honest, respectful, unattached, connected, and productive. My thoughts and energy became aligned instead of divided. I came into a conflict integrated and ready to "face the real so that we all may thrive."

Principles:
- Fear divides the "we" to the "I" and the "it," creating a false sense of separation.
- Fear puts the mind into a state of imbalance of less than or more than.
- When living in fear, we become self-forgetting of our wholeness.
- Inner-peace returns the mind into a state of balance, moving us out of the stress response. It moves us from closed to open.
- Once we are at peace, openness and willingness become possible. These are the two ingredients to access new possibilities.
- Once openness and willingness are established, we can ask, "What do I wish to come of this?" Let the heart speak.

What happens when we bump up against a strong internal resistance? What happens when we are having a hard time getting to the roots?

When the problem is big, this indicates we must dig.
Dig for what is true so that we can see possibilities anew.

Now we have explored the power of pivoting, we will cover the process and model for locating unconscious beliefs that lead to resistance, strife, and limitation. I call this process is called the Outcome Model.

TRANSFORMING OUTCOMES

There is the conscious. The unconscious. The subconscious. Coaching works in the realms of the conscious through choice, action, and new awareness. This is the more transactional side of coaching. Coaching also works in the unconscious realms. As we reflect back and invite the client to go deeper, think broader, and explore wider, we help the client uncover what is beneath the surface but not yet in full conscious awareness. This process brings the unconscious into the conscious.

Coaching does not intentionally work in the subconscious realms. This is where a trained therapist can help. The subconscious is the part of the mind/brain where something may be hidden. Any work on the subconscious that happens during coaching is merely a side effect of the inner work the client is doing. In this regard, sometimes the coaching process of becoming integrated and inwardly aligned can have a therapeutic effect on the client even though it is not therapy. Coaching, however, is not therapy and does not replace a need for treatment.

In coaching, we want to go beneath the surface. If we remain at the surface, so will the problems. True transformation happens at the roots. Think about it like this: Our underlying perception of how we view the world as safe/unsafe, lacking/abundant, good/bad, etcetera, fuels our beliefs about the world. Our beliefs fuel our thoughts about the world. Our thoughts fuel our emotional experiences of the world. Our emotions fuel our actions or inactions. What we do, or don't do, is the outcome we experience.

(+) (-) PERCEPTION → BELIEF → THOUGHTS → EMOTIONS → OUTCOMES

The experience then reflects our perceptions and further solidifies our beliefs because our beliefs are reflected back to us in the outcomes we experience. Thus, we have self-fulfilling prophecies. The problem? We typically live at the level of thought and emotion. We live and experience at the level of effect.

The solution? Take pause and move to the cause. When we get to the roots we impact the fruits. Even Jesus spoke of discerning true teachings by their fruits. The fruit and the fruit alone indicate the foundation we stand upon. Fear or love. Lack or abundance. Probability or possibility. Cause or effect.

In the Outcome Model we can see that the foundation of our perceiving self is paramount.

THE GARDEN OF YOUR LIFE	WEEDS	SEEDS
THE OUTCOME	Limited access to possibility	Fuller access to possibility
τ Action / Inaction	Reactive	Responsive
τ Emotions	Negative emotional experience is a warning we are off track or out of alignment.	Positive emotional experience when we are aligned with our values and needs.
τ Conscious Thoughts	Negative thinking	Open and willing
τ Unconscious Beliefs	False and limiting	Empowering and true
τ UNDERLYING PERCEPTION	I am lacking and afraid	I am whole, complete, and resourced.
Principle	Negative is separative.	Positive is causative.

How does this equation play out in everyday life? Or in our client's outcomes?

Below is an example of a person who lived in the box of limitation with the underlying belief: *I am less than*. This lens filtered all they did and limited their access to what was indeed possible for them. This also reflects what happened when they shifted into their heart, their truth, and got a brand-new start.

COACHING	WEEDS	SEEDS
OUTCOME	No promotion	Promotion
τ Action / Inaction	Tentative, half the effort, holding back	Adaptive, creative, go-getting
τ Emotions	Envy, anxiety, uncertainty	Enthusiasm, respect, appreciation
τ Thoughts	"I didn't do a good enough job." "I am lucky I can get by." "I wish I had what it takes."	"Oh, a new challenge! I've got this. I can learn and I'll give it my best."
τ Core Beliefs	"I don't have what it takes but everyone else does."	"I am equally valuable as anyone else in this world."
τ UNDERLYING PERCEPTION	(I am lacking)	(I am whole, complete, and resourced)

This process is like locating the weeds in our heart, thinking, and perceptions of the world we live in. How we relate to the world is how we then experience the world. Our experiences validate our beliefs and this is why people stay stuck for years and decades.

SHIFT THE FOUNDATION – SHIFT THE OUTCOME

CASE STUDY: The client's underlying belief → If I stop accomplishing, then I am not a success.

Thoughts → I must be the best runner! If I stop running, I won't be the epitome of health. I won't succeed. I'll grow weak. I won't win the races.

Emotions → passion, drive to win, urge to keep going

Actions → run, run, run, run, every day, hours a day, run, run, run, run

Outcome → heart attack from over exertion

This is a powerful example of how human perception can run us to life's richness or run us to ruin. In this case, the client became addicted to running. Addictions happen when we carry a single focus that the foundation of our perception fuels. We believe the thing we attach to will give us relief and becomes an idol of false belief.

When I was stuck in stress eating, deep down I believed I didn't have what it took in this world, and I covered the pain up with food. The problem? Food wasn't the cure. I found the cure in my heart, in the truth of who I was at my core.

FROM FALSE TO TRUE

What do we do when we locate an underlying false/limiting belief? We discover faulty thinking through mindful self-awareness.

Remember, the mind is capable of self-deception so we must go deeper for the answers to life's most pressing questions. In truth, a false perception isn't real at all. It is only a perception.

Look at the fruits. You will notice there were little to no fruits when operating from a false/negative/limited perception. Or, if there were any fruits, they were not that great, like the man that had a heart attack.

When we live at the level of cause, we live at the level of creation. We create new outcomes that extend out to a more positive outcome. A new possibility was brought to life! When we have the faulty foundation, a new possibility was blocked or not brought to life, stifled from potential. A heart attack is the absence of health, not the abundance of. So how does one shift towards the true, positive, causative perception? Go into the heart and choose which seeds you wish to impart.

The heart of who you are, the essence of your consciousness, are choices and virtues. Virtues are our superpowers. You get to choose which superpower to engage. What do you wish the possibility to be here? What do you wish to come of this?

Go into the heart for a brand-new start.
Step out of deception and into a new direction.
Declare what is true and you will renew!

RELEASE THE OLD - DECLARE THE BOLD

Establishing a declaration helps us examine our tradeoffs and helps us clearly define what we are saying yes to in life. A declaration has its roots in the perception that "I am whole, complete, and resourced. I am heading into this possibility."

By saying yes to healthy eating
I am saying no to continued weight gain.

By saying no to being told I'm not good enough.
I'm saying yes to my full worth.

Declarations plant a new seed into our future. Affirmations water these seeds allowing them to grow.

What is a declaration?

A declaration is a stake in the ground. We are declaring a direction. We are stating what we value and desire to bring to life. Declarations help us step into our warrior and take a strong stand for the possibility we are moving into.

Examples:

"From here on out, I am prioritizing my health!"
"For the rest of this year, I will live and breathe self-compassion."
"From this moment forward, I will state my truth."
"I am now leading this company consciously!"

What happens when we declare?

→ We align our energy with our heart.

→ We solidify our intentions.

→ We move forward with motivation.

Declarations help us to be done with the old and step into the **BOLD**!

Remember, creating a new neuropathway can be easier than focusing energy on changing the old habit. Crafting a bold declaration fuels your next steps.

Addressing resistance:

Do you fully believe what you declare? When you state your declaration is your energy solid and aligned? If a part of you isn't fully aligned with what you are declaring, the declaration can fall flat or lack momentum. On a scale from one to ten, ten feeling 100% aligned and one feeling only 10% aligned, how would you rate your feelings of alignment?

If there is any twinge of doubt, we want to know what that's about. It could be false belief lingering. The first approach to consider is "fake it until you make it." Keep stating your declaration until you feel it and until any doubts melt away.

The second consideration is to ponder what is truer? In coaching, we can help a client get to a statement that is "as true as it gets." In other words, if stating that "I am 100% confident in everything I do!" and a part of me knows that isn't true, then it is way too big of a stretch. Go to what I call the "access point." For example, if I feel fully aligned with this statement instead: "I am growing in my confidence each day!" then that is my access point.

The more solid the feeling, the quicker the results.

PLUCK THE WEEDS & PLANT NEW SEEDS

Let's say your client shows up and presents a topic that you see as heavy and maybe even potentially outside the scope of coaching. For example, if they face divorce and wish to do a "conscious uncoupling" process. They show up for their coaching session with you, and their agenda is to determine their needs as they go through the uncoupling and divorce process. As you dive into the session, you observe their mind is ruminating over this. They are sharing how unjust their spouse has been. You find that you inwardly agree that what they are sharing does seem unfair.

You continue to listen, and before you know it, you are getting sucked into the problem with them.

It is one thing to explore the weeds. It is another to get caught in the weeds with your client and accidentally join them in the problem. If you feel like you are joining a client in the problem, be cautious. It is a trap. When someone joins us in the weeds it feels really good. They collude and sympathize with us, and we feel validated. We then feel more justified.

The trap? The perspective that is keeping them stuck is still active. The solution is never found in the actual problem. The solution is found on the other side of the problem, in a different new perspective.

If the client feels validated and justified in their current mindset, the odds of them finding the new empowered perspective minimizes. While it may feel good to the client to join them in the problem, we are doing them a huge disservice when we do. We cannot both be in the problem and help our client get out of the problem. We cannot agree with the problem and help our client dispel the problem.

My mentor Sandy used to say, "I am not a feel-good coach. If someone wants to walk away feeling good, they can go to someone else. I'm here for their greatest good and sometimes the truth is not easy to face, but then it sets you free."

Translation: It feels good to have someone justify our "weeds" and problems as we see them; however, as we bring our clients to view life's weeds from a higher perspective, the solutions surface and the problem no longer binds them.

The client may also benefit from weed-pulling, which is when we help the client identify false beliefs so that they can pluck them out and replace them with more empowering true beliefs. If life were a garden, what would you want to grow?

The issue is that weeds cannot be pulled if we are in them; we need to be just above them to effectively pull them. We also need to see when a weed is a weed.

This is the difference between getting in the weeds and going to the weeds. When we get in the weeds, we join them in the problem. When we go to the weeds, we can observe how they are getting in the way, how our client is relating to them, and help the client:

Pluck the weeds
and plant new seeds!

Steps to take if you feel pulled into the weeds with your client:
1. Take a deep breath to regroup.
2. Remember: "Maybe."
3. Neutralize: Be curious about the person, not the issue. What is in their heart?
4. Empathize: "I am so sorry you are going through this. How can I best support you right now?"
5. Ask open-ended invitations to a new perspective in the direction of their agenda. (See "Birds-Eye View" below.)

Remaining neutral is imperative so that we can coach the client's relationship to the issue and not stay within the limitations of the issue itself.

Notice if you are coaching the issue versus the client's relationship to the issue. Notice what getting pulled in the weeds feels like. Then you can catch yourself. Notice what helps you get to neutral if you do get pulled in.

Watering the Seed:
Once we have a strong declaration in place, we have planted a new seed in our life. To water it means we give it focus, positive attention, and we affirm it. Some people affirm daily, multiple times a day, or weekly, or quarterly. It depends on how much growth we are going for. Our declaration can be our affirmation. Or, we can create other affirmations that help us in different situations to uphold our declaration. For example, if I am working on leadership, I declare: "I am a bold visionary!"

Some of my affirmations to my declaring may be:
- *"I speak up with pride."*
- *"I lead with the end in mind."*
- "My focus in meetings is *respect.*"

I am an introvert and was asked to speak for the Wellness Council. I was nervous because it was a group that was larger to which I was accustomed. My declaration:

"I am a captivating and inspiring speaker!" My affirmation: "This isn't a keynote to 350 people; this is just a speech to a cozier group of 50. If I can do 25, I can do 50. It is all the same." It may sound silly, but it worked. My affirmation reminded me that it wasn't a crazy big step, just a new step.

Go with what is true
and it will see you through.

FUN THEORY

We can also invite integration in fun ways!

Volkswagen conducted social experiments and found that when an element of fun was added to a task that was normally considered not as fun, the fun helped instill a positive new behavior. This just makes sense! They called their discoveries "fun theory."

Fun can create a playful way to create a new neuropathway. In coaching, we have the freedom to be creative. We do not have to be taskmasters, pushing the client into action. Instead, can we be more playful and even have fun? What can you do to invite your client to have fun with a new task? Or to have more fun in your sessions? Just for fun, hop on YouTube and look up fun theory by Volkswagen.

Enjoy!

CHAPTER EIGHT

ଞ Coaching to Integration ଓ

I was first introduced to the concept of integration in college. My psychology teacher was speaking to the concept. I didn't get it. I thought, *I am who I am. How can I integrate further? I am already me.*

Yet, it bothered me that this concept just didn't click and I kept trying to crack the code of this thing called "integration." I'm glad I didn't give up. What I learned is that integration is the fabric of all physical reality and is at the heart of human potential. Integrative coaching invites integration of a client's full human capacity.

Did you know that a goldfish grows to the size of its fishbowl? Human beings are similar. We grow and expand according to the size of our mindsets. We are capable of the greatest innovations or we are capable of the biggest destructions and have the capacity to

develop all of our capacities. We can expand our gifts and abilities. We can see beyond the now and understand the how. We live through vision and develop our skills with precision.

In Chapter Eight, we wrap up with an exploration of coaching to integration. We will examine what it means to be an integratively intelligent coach, the power perception and belief, how to relate to duality, how to identify when an asset turns into a liability, and the gateways to wisdom.

THE INTEGRATIVELY INTELLIGENT COACH

An integratively intelligent coach engages wholeness, connects dots, and helps their client close internal gaps. In this next segment, we will look at the essential qualities of coaching integratively in ways that elevate the human potential embedded within your client.

in·te·gra·tive
/ˈintəɡrādiv/
    adjective
Serving or intending to unify separate things. Oxford Languages

in·te·gra·tion
/ˌin(t)əˈɡrāSH(ə)n/
Noun
  1. The action or process of integrating. Oxford Languages

Integrative coaching accomplishes three things. It engages the whole person, empowers all aspects of life, and elevates potential.

"Engages the whole person" means we do not just coach the problem; we engage the whole person in the self-inquiry process. We coach by engaging the mind with new ways of thinking, the body with new ways of experiencing inner-truth, and the human spirit to lead the way.

"Empowers all aspects" means that we consider all of the areas in life that are interconnected and impacted by what is going on for the client when we are coaching them. We understand that an issue in one area impacts other areas. We also understand that locating a solution in one area can help empower other areas. We see the inter-and inner-connectivity of our client's lives.

"Elevates potential" means that we are inviting our clients to develop as they move towards their goals. There are 8 Domains humans have the capacity to develop. Integrative coaching helps our clients to expand their capacity in each domain, not just one or two.

To understand the full power of integration, let's begin the journey by exploring the key coaching practices that invite integration.

WHOLE PERSON ENGAGEMENT

We have covered coaching to wholeness. Now we are going to explore how to engage a client's wholeness to invite client integration.

Engaging the wholeness of our client, as discussed earlier, is important because questions alone only get us so far. Questions primarily engage the domain of cognitive intelligence. There are seven more intelligences we can invite integration of.

Questions only get us so far.
Masterful coaches engage all domains
to invite full integration.

In masterful coaching, we know that the answers are kept throughout the entirety of the domains of intelligence, not just in one domain. Coaching the whole person means we are coaching each domain of intelligence. Personal trainers know this concept is mirrored in the body. If one muscle is injured, the muscles around it take over and step in to compensate.

When one domain is overused, we can engage the others to step in and be a support.

How aware are you of your client's full range of capacity? Somatically, cognitively, emotionally, energetically, relationally, motivationally, spiritually, and integrationally? Think of these domains as a full spectrum of pathways available to you to enhance your impact. We will explore each of these in-depth when we dive further into the contexts and approaches of integration.

ACCESSING THE WORLD OF POSSIBILITY

Get this! We don't create possibilities. Possibility already exists. It surrounds us twenty-four hours a day, seven days a week, 365 days a year. The bigger question is: "Do we have full access to possibly?"

Possibility = That which can be, exist, or happen.

Through our habits, we create probability around whether or not we have access to the world of possibilities that exist around us.

Probability = The relative possibility that an event will occur.
What we do 90% of the time is what matters. Are we living in possibility or probability? How much *access* we have depends on where our habitual ways of being are located. Blockages:

- False perception
- Negative thoughts/beliefs
- Self-imposed limits
- Fears
- Giving our power away

Closed or fixed mindset
- Openings:
- True perception
- Positive thoughts/beliefs
- Being open and willing
- Cultivating faith
- Keeping power intact
- Open or growth mindset

With blockages, our probability for possibility goes way down.

A basic example of this is at work. If I show up reactive and maintain low levels of willingness, how likely will it be that I will get a promotion? I have engaged in low levels of probability.

However, if I show up to work and I am consistently willing, self-reflective, and attentive, how likely will it be I'll get a promotion? The odds go way up in my favor, and I've amplified my probability something will happen. My habitual way of being, gave me access to the possibility.

We create probability through our habitual ways of being and engage in possibility through opportunity. Why struggle when we can transform barriers into stepping stones? In coaching, we hold the space for possibility when the client is stuck in probability. Again, would you prefer to leave life up to chance or choice?

Peter Drucker says, "The best way to predict the future is to create it." Awareness of our choices, habits, and impact are the catalyst to expanding our personal power and self- agency. If a client is stuck in "no," can you help them locate the "maybe?" When a person is under stress, the brain starts to default to black-and-white thinking, and it can feel as if we don't have a choice. The problem is that nothing in life is black and white. Life is also a full spectrum of color and options.

"Between stimulus and response there is a space.
In that space is our power to choose our response.
In our response lies our growth and our freedom."
- Viktor E. Frankl

In coaching, we help our clients get in touch with the world of possibilities that surround them.

HUMAN VIRTUE

The Sufi tradition teaches that God has ninety-nine virtues evoked when called upon or prayed for. These virtues are all possibilities. Virtues like generosity, compassion, wisdom, love, patience, humility, loyalty, courage, perseverance, etcetera, are all possibilities. We can activate any virtue as we need. Yet, only if we choose to. When we live into our fullest potential, we learn how to activate parts of ourselves that end up being the salve and medicine to our life. If I move out of probability and into possibility, I'm living with intention. I participate in the outcome.

What do you wish to be the possibility of as a coach? As a friend? As a colleague?

As a mother, I wish to be the possibility of love and empowerment. As a coach, I wish to be the possibility of possibility, nurturing, and aligned action. As a leader, I wish to be the possibility of humility, quality, and care.

When there is a challenge, what do you wish to be the possibility of? If your team is clashing, what do you wish to take a stand for? If your kids are giving each other the cold shoulder, what would you wish to demonstrate or teach them? When a friend keeps nagging you, what type of space do you wish to hold? As human beings, we have the option to find our true selves so that we can then choose who we wish to be.

Chance or choice? It is in our hands and master coaches invite clients to active the possibilities within them.

NAVIGATING THE RABBIT HOLE OF PERCEPTION

> *"Reality is the actuality of that which is real and true.*
> *Reality includes everything that is and has been,*
> *whether or not it is observable or comprehensible."*
> *-Wikipedia*

Reality is a philosophical inquiry that we won't be questioning today; however, in coaching it is wise to ask, "In what ways do we experience reality?" Understanding the full human experience helps us masterfully respond to our client's feelings and needs.

There are three ways we can take in and experience reality.

- Rationally: Logical. Factual. Measurable. Observable.
- Non-rationally: Does not make logical sense and yet is true. Intangible. Not always observable. Felt-sense. "More to life than meets the eye."
- Irrationally: Appears to be real and is not. Illusion.

Rational experience is easy to perceive intellectually. Irrational experiences are false interpretations of reality, also perceived by the intellect. The non-rational side of life experience either gets brushed aside or overlooked because... well, it just isn't logical, and it isn't always wrapped in a tidy little package.

Rational coaching approaches:	Non-rational coaching approaches:
<ul><li>Time management</li><li>Strategy</li><li>Affirmation</li><li>Belief shifting</li><li>Assessments</li></ul>	<ul><li>Somatic inquiry</li><li>Emotional feedback</li><li>Guided meditation</li><li>Metaphor exploration</li><li>Intuitions</li></ul>

Masterful coaching blends
the rational and non-rational,
while dispelling the irrational.

In a masterful coaching session, we can use the non-rational to locate the rational. We weed through the irrational to get grounded back in the rational. If a client is stuck looping in their thinking, you can toss in a non-rational exercise. This acts as a pattern disrupt and allows the client to access answers without overthinking stumping their progress.

Non-rational approaches mirror what we need but may not be aware we need it. They can snap us into new ways of embracing and relating to "what is" so we can reset the direction we are going to choose next.

Let's take a moment to explore the full capacity of what the non-rational experiences of reality have to offer our clients and how they can empower your coaching. Many people, whether or not they believe in a higher power, report experiences that defy logic. People experience everything from spiritual awakenings to intuitions that defy scientific explanations and blow logic out of the water.

I was reading an article about a brain surgeon who had a higher-than-normal success rate with his surgeries. He admitted he didn't know how or why he was so much better than his colleagues. When he was in surgery, he reported what to do next just intuitively came to him; he reported sensing parts of the brain as if the brain would light up for him and show him the way. Following his intuition led to the highest levels of precision and a precision that defied both logic and probability. He didn't understand how his intuition was possible but learned to trust it. As a result, he was able to save thousands of lives.

Have you ever experienced something that defied logic but left an impression on you?

When I was in my twenties, I had a "more than meets the eye experience." I had decided I was an atheist in my teens. Atheism felt safe and logical. Growing up, my parents took us to church occasionally, but they didn't believe in God, so I decided religion was man-made and left it at that. I also decided to believe that if something couldn't be physically measured, it didn't exist. I was at a point in my life when I was a single mom and struggling with emotional eating from the stress of it all. One day I hit rock bottom. I had just eaten a box of crackers and half a pizza out of complete stress. I felt so numb, empty, and hopeless afterward. I laid down on the bed and couldn't stop asking, "What is wrong with me?" over and over. That one question permeated my mind.

I eventually decided to get up. I wandered over to a bookcase in my mother's room. I was looking for a distraction. I plopped down on the floor next to one of many large bookcases. This bookcase housed hundreds of books. My eyes landed on a random book by Susan Jeffers entitled, *Feel the Fear and Do It Anyway*. I had never heard of it. I pulled it out. Why not. Any book would help at this point. I opened the book to a "random" page instead of starting on page one. My eyes were caught by a "random" question the author posed in the middle of the introduction. It read verbatim, "This should be a relief to all of you out there who have been wondering, 'What is wrong with me?'"

I gasped and then burst out in tears. What just happened? I was so confused. Out of all of the bookcases my mom had, I happened to plop down next to that bookcase. Out of the hundred books in that bookcase, I happened to notice that one book out of all four shelves of random books. Out of all the pages I could have randomly opened to, I opened to a random page that answered the question I just asked.

What are the odds?! I couldn't explain any of it.

My experience defied probability more than once. Three times to be exact. I decided to become agnostic after that point, and I realized there is much more to life than meets the eye, even if it was unexplainable. I have since learned that these non-rational moments provide interesting shortcuts for people. In John C. Maxwell's book, *21 Irrefutable Laws of Leadership*, he concluded that intuition was one of the key laws to effective leadership. He points out that effective leaders know how to trust their gut.

How much do you trust your gut as a coach?

As we coach, we need to be aware that:
- Rational ways of knowing can be limited and limiting.
- Non-rational ways of knowing can lead to shortcuts.
- Both keep each other in check. The goal is to stay out of the irrational.

Non-rational knowing brought into rational awareness can help ground an intuition.

→ Example: "I have a strong sense that if I quit my job all will be OK. What steps can I take to do this the smart way, though?"

Rational "knowing" when run by intuition can be double-checked.

→ Example: "I say I want the promotion, but my stomach churns every time I bring it up. What is that about?"

Rational knowing and non-rational knowing are both avenues to help the client examine truth from illusion and get out of traps found in the irrational. This allows the client to shed self-deception and lead a life empowered from within.

Examples of engaging the rational side of our clients all have to do with engaging mental cognition:
  • Facts / Observations
  • Words / Agreements
  • Goals / Action
  • Mindset / Beliefs

Examples of engaging the whole person by including non-rational aspects of our clients, moving them beyond mental cognition:
  • Intuitions
  • Feelings
  • Emotions
  • Sensations
  • Impressions
  • Imagination
  • Imagery / Vision
  • Desires / Callings

As you can see, this approach is all-inclusive and integrates the power of the mind, body, and human spirit. Masterful coaches engage the whole person.

Don't forget, we are sentient beings capable of abstract thought. We are capable of comprehending great truths. Think Gandhi and Dr. Martin Luther King Jr. Or, on the other hand, we can create empires upon illusion. Think Hitler.

Examples of Irrational:
- o FEARS = False evidence appearing really scary
- o Assumptions
- o False Perceptions
- o Illusions
- o Mindset Pitfalls

MOVING FROM EFFECT TO CAUSE

One of our jobs as a coach is to help our clients live empowered. To grasp empowerment, we are wise to learn the principles and power behind words.

"Let us not forget, however, that words are but symbols of symbols.
They are thus twice removed from reality."
- A Course in Miracles

This is because:

Reality is. Reality includes what is, what has been, and what is possible. Our interpretation of reality places us once removed from reality. Our judgment of our interpretation then places us twice removed from reality.

And if we keep going down the rabbit hole we see just how far self-deception's tentacles can spread over a lifetime. Every judgment of a judgment adds another layer of self- deception. If we judge interpretations against other external interpretations, like media or family belief systems, we can be four to five times removed from reality.

All of the layers are just illusions, padding us from reality. This fragmenting off from reality happens when we become scared of reality, where we've judged it as unsafe.

The problem? Living, thinking, believing away from reality places us in the land of interpretations and complicates our assumptions. The further away, the more we stay... stuck. Being layers removed from reality takes our power away, placing us at the level of effect in our lives. Nothing can't produce something. Truth can't produce illusion. Illusion can't produce truth.

We can live at the level of cause or effect.
To live at the cause,
we go back to the source and choose a better course.

The farther we live removed from reality, the more struggle ensues, the more negative life feels and therefore becomes harder and heavier. Illusions exist because they seem so real and that is how we remain self-deceived inside the boxes our mind has constructed.

Living fully present to reality, places us at the level of cause. Living removed from reality, places us at the level of effect.

As we begin to self-examine, to awaken to reality, we naturally begin to put down the layers of illusions we've packed on over the years. When we come back home to ourselves, we live at the level of cause. True empowerment is not power over. It is power from within.

Powerful coaching empowers the client. Powerful coaching moves the client from living at the effect to creating their life at the level of cause.

BEYOND THE WORDS

Words may be removed from reality, but they echo and reflect what is beneath the surface. A truth or an illusion. Words have the ability to activate new possibilities because of what they represent.

Masterful coaches choose words potent with possibility!
- What if…
- What else?
- Where is your power in this?
- In what ways can this be easy?
- What part of you believes this is possible?

As you are working with your clients, you may notice their words and interpretations. Notice if their words are keeping them trapped and invite freedom. Notice if their words are keeping them limited and invite expansion. Notice if their language is negative and invite the positive.

> *"The words, then, are symbols for the things asked for,*
> *but the things themselves but stand for*
> *the experiences that are hoped for."*
> *- A Course in Miracles*

EMBRACING DUALITY

There is a saying in Sufism:

> *"May the face of the Real be upon you."*

This is perhaps what the Christian saying "May God be with you" means. Or in *Star Wars*, "Use the Force, Luke."

It also symbolizes the state of non-deception, where we see clearly. Peeking at life through the lens of integrative intelligence, we include all aspects that serve a greater good.

 A powerful symbol for how we experience duality is depicted in the Taoist philosophy and ancient Chinese symbol of the yin-yang. This symbol represents "a concept of dualism, describing how seemingly opposite or contrary forces may be complementary, interconnected, and interdependent in the natural world, and how they may give rise to each other as they interrelate to one another."(18)

It also symbolizes the concept that anything negative can always transform into something positive, and that anything positive has the potential transform into something negative. We must be aware of these potentials.

The yin-yang also speaks to life's dualities:
- Positive / Negative
- Inhale / Exhale
- Masculine / Feminine
- Rational / Non-rational

Masterful coaches embrace duality.

If my client gets fired, we must not forget that something better is now possible for them. In thinking there is something better, we must not forget that there was first pain and loss. It is both. It is duality. As integrative coaches, we may also feel and hold space for a multitude of conflicting emotions. If I am going to start a new job, I may feel both excited and nervous. It is both. Yet, if I only focus on the excitement, I may forget that nervousness can remind me how I want to show up prepared. If I only focus on the nervousness, I may forget the positive aspect and show up stressed out.

As a coach, we hold a larger space that is fully inclusive of all that is. As we hold a larger space, we hold is a potentiated space. Paulo Coelho's book, The Alchemist, tells a tale of a wise man teaching a boy about wisdom. He gives the boy a spoon with oil in it, tells him not to spill the oil, and then sends him out to see the wonders of the world. Upon the boy's return, the oil was there, but he couldn't speak to the wonders of the world. The wise man sends the boy out again, instructing him to notice the wonders of the world. This time boy comes back with an empty spoon. The wise man tells the boy, "The secret of happiness is to see all the marvels of the world and never forget the drops of oil on the spoon."

Go out in the world and never be too distracted to remember what is important. Go out into the world and never be so focused that you forget to embrace the miracles surrounding you along your journey.

Integration includes all that is deemed good, bad, positive, and negative. They all serve when we are aware.

EXAMINING ASSETS & LIABILITIES

BFF #1 - "I can't leave him."

BFF #2 - "Why not."

BFF #1 - "It will hurt him."

BFF #2 - "You've called me crying at least weekly about how emotionally abusive he has been."

BFF #1 - "He is teaching me how to be a stronger person and the triggers I need to heal."

At what point do human virtues such as empathy or compassion keep us entrapped? When does the human asset turn into a human liability?

My mentor Sandy called it. She loved to say, "Different times, different things." When does compassion become too much compassion and morph boundaries or have us abandon our needs? When does stress motivate us and at what point does it hamper us with exhaustion? When is an axiom a lantern of truth and when does it no longer pertain?

ax·i·om

/ˈaksēəm/

noun

"A statement or proposition which is regarded as being established, accepted, or self-evidently true." - Oxford Languages

Below are some common axioms. Notice the dual nature of asset and liability.

No pain, no gain.
- o ASSET: Helpful when working out.
- o LIABILITY: Potentially harmful when in a relationship.

Waste not, want not.
- o ASSET: Financial wealth.
- o LIABILITY: Financial stinginess.

Sticks and stones break bones. Words can never hurt me.
- o ASSET: To shake off a verbal attack as a kid.
- o LIABILITY: To overlook the need for empathy.

An idle mind is a waste.
- o ASSET: To increase productivity.
- o LIABILITY: When a mental break is needed.

Distractions kill productivity.
- o ASSET: When we need to focus to finish.
- o LIABILITY: When piddling around invites innovation.

Love is blind.
- o   ASSET: When it is time to love unconditionally.
- o   LIABILITY: Looking the other way when a boundary is crossed.

Ice cream makes everything better.
- o   ASSET: When you need a fun break from stress.
- o   LIABILITY: Emotional eating leads to substantial weight gain.

To be an optimist is good. To be a pessimist is bad.
- o   ASSET: When positive thinking gets you past the finish line.
- o   LIABILITY: When you need to look at the negatives to create a better positive.

Viewing life integratively, we can see that life is not black and white, this or that. This teaching is valuable for helping our clients move beyond self-deception. Self-mastery comes from embracing the concept of "different times, different things." Self-mastery roots when we realize how assets can become out of balance.

I was with a friend that was in training to be a yoga instructor. I had the opportunity to join her in her home studio for her practice sessions. We were about half-way through a very vigorous vinyasa flow. Vinyasa is typically a rigorous and non-stop flow from pose to pose. This sequence was so challenging that we stopped to grab water. Usually, in yoga, you push through or take child's pose to rest. This day, we put our glasses of water against the back wall of her studio and then dove back in. I recall doing a pose, I was upside down, and I noticed my glass of water. I was exhausted and pushing through. For some reason, the glass of water kept standing out to me. So, I asked myself the tell-tale question, "Is the glass half empty? Is it half full? What is the highest truth?"

Then it dawned on me.

It is both.

In masterful coaching, we hold dichotomies. We hold paradoxes. We hold space for "maybe." We hold space for yes and no. We do this so our clients can see through limiting assumptions, eliminate self-deception and step into the solidity of their own power.

In one scenario, my judgments made me wrong. In another scenario, my judgments made me strong. How do you hold paradox? How do you help your clients hold paradox?

A CAVEAT TO POSITIVE THINKING

Is positive thinking always positive? People and cultures go through fads. A fad that has taken off is around positive thinking. What could be bad about positive thinking? After all, it is positive!

As we've seen, everything can be an asset or turn into a liability. While people benefit greatly from being positive, we want to be conscious of what stream we are swimming in. Am I open to possibility? Or am I living an illusion that everything is fine when it isn't?

One of my bosses over the years was fascinating to me. He started each day with a spiritual saying. I thought, "Wow, what a positive person!" I felt so inspired by him. I hadn't seen many bosses that were so thoughtful. Yet, this boss had a reputation for being "wishy- washy." Let's call him Jim for the sake of the story.

In my initial interview for the position, I was told, "I think you would be a great fit. I'd like to offer you the position, but can you say no to Jim?" Jim was the owner of the business that held the job I was applying to. He was going to be my boss. He had a reputation for doing whatever he wanted at the moment and put a positive spin on everything. In other words, if anyone approached Jim upset, Jim would fix it by offering a positive solution. Sounds great, right?! Well, the solution completely ignored policies and government regulations under which the business was operating. This would happen two to three times per week. The staff would then put out the fires as best they could.

He was so positive that he couldn't see why this was an issue. When you don't follow government regulations, that is a problem if you want to stay in business. Also, when a state law is ignored, that is a legal liability risk. Or, if a policy was ignored for one person and not another, that is an equality issue.

After four years of cleaning up the "positive thinking" messes, and an unwillingness to look at the impact of his rosy mindset, I turned in my resignation.

The way out is through.
Truth is our greatest shortcut.

We want to be open to possibilities, but wouldn't true positive thinking include all angles, including the so-called "negative"? If we lean too far into pie-in-the-sky thinking, we can fall into self-deception just as much as negative thinking. Avoidance has a consequence.

Ignoring issues in many cases exacerbates the problem, or at a minimum, solves nothing.

Can we embody both the positive and negative? Yes. Can we be grounded in what is true? Are we willing to look at all angles? Can I see how genuine positivity is inclusive of all of the "good," "bad," "right," and "wrong"? Can I catch myself minimizing, ignoring, or putting on rosy goggles under the guise of "positive thinking"?

Sometimes have to go through the muck in order to get unstuck.

EXPLORING THE GATEWAYS TO OUR WISDOM
"What you think, you create. What you feel, you attract.
What you imagine, you become."
- Rhonda Byrne

We have a mind; the human intellect, our consciousness.
We have a body; the soma, our physicality.
We have a human spirit; the heart, our highest self.

These are the three centers of human knowing. These are also sometimes these are also referred to as the Centers of Wisdom or ways we know. The goal is to live in balance with our mind, body and spirit. We balance these centers by aligning them in proper order.

Alignment is vastly overlooked. Most people attempt to balance the centers horizontally. Example: Mind – Body – Spirit. I believe this has placed an unconscious emphasis on the mind being in the lead. This carries consequences and can feed imbalances.

True balance of the centers is attainable through alignment, better understood vertically. Each part has its place and purpose. We will be looking through the lens of alignment.

Optimized alignment looks more like this:
    Spirit (inner compass leads)
    Mind (is optimized when brought into alignment with spirit and body)
    Body (grounds us, allows us to act and experience)

These three centers are ways to embody wisdom. However, there is a pitfall, though. We also have an ego. Did you notice the ego didn't make the list as a center of knowing? The ego is the aspect of the mind based on fear and is the consequence of giving the mind in a leadership role. The ego effectively pinches off human potential. Let's examine the role the ego plays in human psychology so that you can fully understand what your clients are up against.

THE EGO

The egoic self is the gatekeeper that blocks the doorways to our deepest wisdom. The good news is the ego cannot solve the problems of the ego. This is also bad news. The ego relentlessly attempts to solve the problems it generates… until we become self-aware, that is. The opposite of the ego would be the highest self, our inner compass. Egoic extrapolations are only that extrapolations. The ego's only basis is an illusion, and it constructs defense mechanisms to keep us "safe."

Wholeness can never be found in fragmented stories of the egoic self. The ego equates itself with the body and disregards the heart. It survives only in the machinations of the mind, in our thinking and interpretations. The ego's attempts to keep us safe become the very bars that ultimately limit and imprison us. The ego is the inner-critic, and without an ego there would be no inner-critic to contend with.

What about the body then? We live in our body. Yet, you are more than your body. The body is neutral. It reflects what it needs physically, what thoughts you think, and what you feel as a result of your thoughts. The body issues cues. The ego takes those cues and twists them into quite a variety of defenses and safety mechanisms. The catch? The body reacts just as much to an illusion as it does to the truth.

Self-mastery is full awareness of the egoic self so that we can pivot to true self. When we lead life through egoic fear, negative thoughts will appear. When we lead life through love, we rise above.

Fear is only a state of mind.
Love is a state of being.

Which lens are you looking through life with? The ego, the body, the mind or the heart? Your body will reflect back to you the lens you are looking through. The body is not capable of deception, just reflection. The deception comes from the interpretations of the mind.

Taking the power that the mind has to generate a truth or illusion for granted is nothing to take lightly. The mind is the inception point of creation. Look around your current home.

Your home, the items you are surrounded by, were first a thought before they became a thing.

Who's in the lead? Who's in charge? Which voice speaks louder? Placing the mind in allegiance to the heart is the beginning of a very powerful start. An atheist asked a rabbi, "How do you know God exists?" The rabbi asked back, "What are the odds that if I spill this jar of ink that it will spill onto the paper as a beautiful poem?" The agnostic replied, "None."

I am not suggesting God exists or doesn't exist. This is for you to decide for yourself. I am suggesting that the mind is the inception point of new creation in the physical world and is due its respectful place. Since the mind is capable of self-deception, we are wise to become self-aware. Here is a perspective of the journey we take into our wholeness.

Let's take a journey through the gateways.

Within the heart,
the birth of wisdom has a start.

Within the mind,
fears and illusions, we shall find.

The mind, riddled with self-deception,
has us creating more and more protection.

Once we move beyond self-deception,
we then find the heart of all true connection.

Steering life through the mind
is how our heart ends up blind.

Steering life through the heart
is where joy and fulfillment do start.

The body acts like a mirror,
reflecting to us the direction we chose to steer.

The body is gateway one,
reflecting to us when self-awareness has begun.

The mind is gateway number two.
When properly used helps us shed the untrue.

The third and final gateway appears
once we decide to relinquish limitations and fears.

Opening to our heart is gateway number three.
Here truth and kindness set us free.

Coming home to live illuminated in our own heart
Is all we ever longed for from the start.

Home is where the heart is.

The heart carries a blueprint of our truths. When we tune in and listen, it steers us like a compass. Helping your clients perceive from their hearts is powerful. The heart is the client's highest asset. I've never met one person who does not have a heart to them. We all carry higher wisdom within. The question is, are we in touch with this most powerful part of self?

Just turn on the news to discover the answer is most likely no.

To be balanced in mind-body-spirit is to honor the purpose and function of each. Many people place these in an order that leads to self-deception.

A Course in Miracles teaches that the ego's voice is loud and boisterous. The heart is quiet and knowing. To begin to hear our inner wisdom, we must first get at peace. Once we are at peace, the heart does speak.

When our client comes to us frantic, we can help them stop, drop into their heart, and roll into a new perspective. This calms the body. I call this process: stop, drop, and roll.

The mind is highly susceptible to self-deception and lives through evaluations, thus twice removed from reality. The heart is intuitive, capable of wisdom, virtue, inner-knowing, and love. Your heart is the virtue of you and connects mind, body, and spirit.

Place the mind in allegiance to the heart
and what you are capable of creating will be brilliantly smart.

THE FIRST GATEWAY - THE BODY

The body is brilliant!

The body issues feedback that is not always rational. This is how the body reports self- deception. The questions are, are we listening so that the body becomes a grounding ally? A coach who understands the nature and role of the body can take their clients to the next level in their self-awareness. The body's feedback mechanisms include feelings and sensations: hunger, fullness, thirst, nutritional needs, need for rest, sickness, wounding, and intuitions. It also issues feedback emotionally: sad, happy, angry, scared, or elated.

Feelings and sensations also include constriction, body temperature, tension, and energy heightened or lost. When I was a personal trainer I learned how the body issues hunger cues when it needs more fuel. The body also issues signals when it has had enough to eat.

The body is the home to our heart, our mind, and our energy. The body is also generative. If I think a thought, real or perceived, the body generates an emotional response. To live and coach masterfully, we can learn to incorporate the feedback the body is issuing. The body stores memory, reflects what we believe, and reminds us what has happened to us in the past. If we are aware, the body can play an instrumental role in helping us locate illusions, facilitate healing, navigate us back to our truth, and is how we take action.

There is wisdom in understanding the nature of physical limitation. If I need to rest and I override this need for too long, the mind may begin to hallucinate and lose acuteness. (16) If I injure myself and do not allow time for healing, I may cause more damage. On the inverse, when I had a level-three sprained ankle, I was advised to push through the pain of physical therapy to avoid scar tissue from forming.

There is a time to heal. A time to feel.
There is a time to push through. A time to renew.
There is a time to eat. A time to retreat.

A key component to self-mastery is learning how to engage the mind and body connection. The mind is powerful, can alter the perceived limitations of the body, and leads to a stronger, more resilient body. Studies have shown that the mind can impact muscle tissue. One study by Brian Clark at Ohio University found:

"Clark and colleagues recruited twenty-nine volunteers and wrapped their wrists in surgical casts for an entire month. During this month, half of the volunteers thought about exercising their immobilized wrists. For eleven minutes a day, five days a week, they sat completely still and focused their entire mental effort on pretending to flex their muscles. When the casts were removed, the volunteers that did mental exercises had wrist muscles that were two times stronger than those that had done nothing at all." (13)

261

I recall an arduous backcountry hike. I headed out the night before, camped, ate a light dinner. I woke at dawn after little rest, ate the rest of the food, and headed out. I trekked up steep hills encased in slippery dirt that loved to dissipate under our feet like sand. I descended over 200 feet of steep mountainside terrain into a deep valley floor full of water, rocks, dragonflies, and turtles. The canyon was beautiful! Yet, I was miserable.

The problem? I was running on little sleep, I ran out of water, I had eaten the last food rations and had hiked in heavy climbing gear in the hopes there was some climbing to find. The gear was heavy and the desert sun unforgiving and scalding hot. I found pockets of stagnant water in the canyon. Undrinkable. I wet my clothes each time I came across a water hole, only to be dry again in two minutes from the scorching heat. Then I determined, "I have to get back out." I was physically exhausted, mentally drained from the lack of sleep, hungry, thirsty, and felt my body struggling to keep going. Yet, the only safety was to make it back to the car.

Trekking out was twenty times harder than trekking in. Every step felt like my legs were weighted with bricks. My lips were chapped, my mouth was growing drier with each minute, my skin burning, my stomach growling. The more my mind turned to fear, the harder it became to keep going. I decided to buck up and get myself back to safety. Speaking stopped. There was one mission: Make it safely back to the car.

I allowed my heart to decide I wanted to be safe and make it home. I took control of my mind by placing it in allegiance to the goal. Instead of fear, I choose thoughts like: I got this! Push through. I'm gaining strength. I am strong and in control.

When my thoughts were clear, intentional, and strong, my body responded with more energy. It never became easy, but the push became doable. I also noticed my mind would begin to slip back into fear and lack. I caught myself feeling even heavier and more exhausted. I caught myself thinking: I'm so thirsty, I'm starving. This is horrible. I am not going to make it. I feel trapped.

As I shifted the focus of my mind, my body followed suit like clockwork.

I did make it back safely. I had newfound gratitude for the power of the mind/body connection and what my body was capable of when my mind took charge.

Mastery in the somatic domain comes from understanding the clues and cues the body is giving us. Mastery is respecting the body as a sacred aspect of our life experience.

so·mat·ic
/səˈmadik/
adjective
1. "Relating to the body, especially as distinct from the mind." Oxford Languages

As we grow somatically aware, we begin to understand what the body is telling us, how it delivers information, and the ways it reflects both the conscious and unconscious.

I once came across a book entitled, *Be Careful What You Think. Your Body Will Believe You.* I never read it because I felt the title said it all. Think about it! The body is at the center for perceiving and experiencing reality. We see, feel, and sense all through the body. The body is the centrifuge of all we do and is an expression of who we choose to be. When we understand the role the body plays in our self-awareness journey and use it as feedback to where we are in alignment or out of alignment, we expand our capacity for mastery.

SOMATIC AWARENESS

Somatic coaching includes the body as a feedback mechanism to help clients gauge when they are on track or off track. Self-awareness around the body's responses act as an instrument for feedback reflecting both the conscious and unconscious aspects of self.

Some examples of what to look for when coaching:

- Vocal shifts: pacing, tone
- Facial expressions: tears, smiling, flushed expressions, eye movement
- Body sensations: tension, breath rate, heart rate, temperature
- Energy sensations: butterflies in my stomach, empty hole in the heart
- Posture: hand/feet placement, hand gestures, seated or standing stances

The mind is capable of self-deception. The body is not. The body reflects what is or has happened to us physically, emotionally, or mentally. It reflects responses to what a client is thinking, feeling, sensing, and emoting (hormones released). It reflects both the conscious and unconscious.

Somatic coaching
integrates the rational and non-rational
while dispelling the irrational.

RETURNING TO A NEUTRAL OBSERVER

Sometimes the body can feel so deeply, our emotional reaction can sway the mind. "I am crying heavily. I must be inconsolable. This situation is going to take me under." The mind can make up stories about the body's feedback until we become aware of truth versus an illusion and become a neutral observer. Being a neutral observer of somatic response allows us to rise above the reaction and not create a story that may be untrue.

Biases observer: "Oh, no. I feel anxious. Something is wrong."

Neutral observer: "Oh, interesting. That phone call left me feeling anxious. I wonder what that is about?"

Coaching as neutral observer: "When you spoke of feeling anxious after the phone call, where does the jump to "something is wrong" come from?"

The body's objectivity is the fundamental gateway to self-awareness by reflecting to us what's beneath the surface.

We can also influence the body to have an experience. For example, when we smile, oxytocin is released. A prominent social psychologist, Amy Cuddy, found that when we hold a strong pose, it helps us feel powerful. She calls these "power poses." So, when I hold a power-pose for two minutes, I feel more aligned and stronger, using my body to experience greater alignment.

ANCHORING IN INSIGHTS

Movement can also help our clients switch gears and anchor in a new perspective. One of my favorite somatic approaches carries this basic rhythm:

1. "Where does this issue show up in your body?"
2. "What does it feel like?"
3. "Does it have a shape or color?"
4. "Does it have a metaphor?"
5. "OK. Are you ok with standing up and shaking the problem off?"
6. You can shake it off with them to help you reset as well.
7. After they are back sitting, invite a few deep breaths.
8. "Let's pretend the solution has already happened. What does the solution "feel" like?" Notice I didn't ask what does it look like. They may not know yet.
9. "Where does the feeling show up in your body?" Stay in somatic feedback.
10. "Does it have a color or shape?"
11. "What virtue does it represent to you?"
12. "Is there a metaphor?"

After we help the client explore what a solution might feel like to them somatically, we can invite them to reverse engineer what a solution might look like.

Below is a case study that represents how a combination of movement, metaphor, and feeling can play out in inviting real-time solutions:

Coach: Hi, Carol, great to see you! Where are we heading today?

Client: I am feeling stuck at work. I'm in my first management role, and it is really triggering a lot of insecurities.

Coach: (after establishing the agenda and fully exploring) So you identified you want to walk away with a new approach for running your staff meetings with our time together today?

Client: Yes!

Coach: How do staff meetings feel right now?

Client: Horrible. I'm tense, I go in feeling unprepared and unsure of myself. Coach: Where do you feel this in your body?
Client: My chest. It is tight and it feels dense for some reason. Coach: Does it have a color?
Client: I would say gloomy grey, or brown like mud, thick mud. Coach: Is there a metaphor that comes to mind?
Client: Sludge! Or, quicksand. It's like there is no movement, or I get sucked in.

Coach: I'm hearing…a density in your chest, gloomy, thick sludge, quicksand, and getting sucked in.

Client: Yes!

Coach: I can imagine you may not enjoy your staff meetings when you feel this way. Client: Nope! (both laugh)
Coach: I completely understand. Are you open to switching gears now? Client: Sure. Coach: I invite you to stand up where you are and really shake the sludge off. I'll do this with you. Shake off the gloom, shake off the dense, the quicksand, and just really let it all go.

Client: OK!

Coach: Let's keep going and when you feel a complete release will you let me know?
Client: Yes. *(a few more moments)* OK! I'm good.

Coach: As you sit back down I invite you to take a few deep breaths with me and even smile. *(Smiling engages the release of positive hormones.14)*

Client: *(client sits, now relaxed, smiling slightly and more open)*

Coach: Let's imagine for a moment that this problem was completely dissolved for you. Imagine you just found the perfect solution. What feelings come up for you?

Client: I feel confident, I feel clear, and I feel grateful for my role. *Coach:* Does the confident, clear, and grateful have a color?
Client: I would say amber, like a sunrise.

Coach: Where does the amber sunrise show up in your body?

Client: *(client takes a moment and tunes into to their body)* It is in my solar plexus, up through my chest and even throat.

Coach: What does showing up in your meeting as the amber sunrise mean to you?

Client: *(client thinks....)* It means I'm showing up self-compassionate *(continues to think)...and I feel prepared...and I'm also ready, eager, and equipped.

Coach: *(observing the client shift into a "yes")* Is this how you want to show up? *(coach checks in to see if the shift is felt by the client)*

Client: Yes! That would be amazing.

Coach: What becomes possible if you show up as the amber sunrise version of yourself?

Client: I think the meetings would go so much smoother! I would also feel so much at ease and hopefully invite more ease. I notice when I'm tense, my team gets tense with me, and I don't want that at all.

Coach: What will help you show up as the amber sunrise, with self-compassion, prepared, ready, eager, and equipped? (only after confirming and acknowledging the shift, the coach invites the exploration of action)

Client: I think if I were to, 1) prepare in advance what the purpose of the meeting is; and then 2) right before the meeting if I did a short mediation and get into the energy of "sunrise" and find ways to inspire.

Coach: What does a sunrise symbolize to you?

Client: Being an inspiration, starting anew, and illuminating.

Coach: Excellent! I feel inspired just listening to you. What are your next steps?

From here, the coach/client wrap up and explore next steps, takeaways, any obstacles, accountability, resources, timelines, and acknowledgments.

To help a client anchor in an insight, invite their "yes" to come through. When the yes isn't yet logical, explore whole-person: feelings, emotions, impressions, and invite what is possible.

> *"Sometimes your joy is the source of your smile,*
> *but sometimes your smile can be the source of your joy."*
> —*Thich Nhat Hanh*

THE SECOND GATEWAY - THE MIND

Let's look at the powerful nature of the human mind. We are alive. We have life. We have choice and the capacity for self-determination. Life replicates. Consciousness chooses.

> *"Consciousness remains one of the most bizarre phenomena*
> *in the universe. Though a well-researched field, science is still*
> *to reveal the fundamental nature of consciousness."*
> *~ Chaos Theory and Consciousness, by Arpan Dey*

Let's look at the mind through a more integrative lens. First, how do we define the mind? Science equates the mind with the physical brain. Is there more to it?

A story was passed down to me about an astronaut who was friends with a brain surgeon. The astronaut said, "You know, I've been to space and back and I've never seen God." The brain surgeon thought about that and replied, "That is interesting. I've done hundreds of brain surgeries, and I've never seen a thought."

Theology often stipulates that the mind is the soul, the energy of who we are that surpasses the body even after death.

Philosophy asks where the mind exists? Are we just a brain, or are we so much more?

Psychology studies the mind and equates the mind in some disciplines as the sum of the thinker. Sigmund Freud was a psychologist and found that certain mindsets, conscious or unconscious, lent to his patients experiencing physical ailments, or helped heal them.

In his book, *Man's Search for Meaning*, Victor Frankl observed a direct mind/body correlative. Dr. Frankl was an Austrian psychiatrist and Holocaust survivor of the concentration of death camps in Germany, WWII. Because of his status as a doctor, he was pulled aside for other duties that allowed him to observe what was going on. He began to observe a pattern: once a person lost hope, they died within three days. He also noticed that those holding onto hope could endure and live through the worst of human atrocities.

In "new age" spiritual thought, the mind is viewed as the interface with the Akashic Records. Akashic is Sanskrit for "Hidden Library." The philosophy is that everything is energy and whenever something happens it leaves an energetic footprint. The belief here is that the mind has the capacity to pick up on energy patterns and time/space do not exist at the level of energy, kind of like how a radio picks up on the radio wave channel. The channel is akin to an event. If you tune into the channel, you can tune into the event.

Interestingly enough, research into quantum physics has discovered very similar findings.

Recall Elizabeth Lloyd Mayer's experience that left her dumbfounded. She used a psychic, or "dowser," to recover her daughter's harp and this challenged her explanation of reality as she knew it. How was this possible since it wasn't measurable? How could a mind pick up on something it knows nothing about? Elizabeth dedicated her life to researching psychic phenomena and learned that both the FBI and CIA have a history of successfully hiring psychics to solve the unsolvable.

When thinking of the mind, are we thinking in a box? Or are we open to the mind being capable of picking up on more than meets the eye? Are we ignoring an entire aspect of our being, our intuitive self? How do our beliefs of what we are, keep us limited?

> *"There are more things in heaven and earth, Horatio,*
> *than are dreamt of in your philosophy."*
> *- Hamlet by Shakespeare*

If we assume the mind is limited, we will be right. If we are open to the mind being so much more, we open to possibility. The minute we define potential, we also limit it. This is the irony of potential. Can we dance in the possibility that we don't know our full capacity? Can we dance in the mystery? Can we expand beyond what we perceive to know?

Definition of the mind for our purposes of understanding and understanding the role the mind plays in coaching is:

Conscious Awareness

The mind is where we think thoughts, interpret, reflect, believe, and make choices through our awareness and consciousness. The mind is powerfully creative, yet is also the home to the egoic self, the part that thinks, "I am me" and "I am separate." The mind is capable of choice, instigating action, and houses beliefs. The mind is the home to the domain of the intellect. The mind, in all of its power to choose and create outcomes, is also the part of us that is the most vulnerable to self-deception and limitation.

Masterful coaches are aware of how the mind is an asset and when the mind becomes a liability.

mind

/mīnd/

noun

1. the element of a person that enables them to be aware of the world and their experiences, to think, and to feel; the faculty of consciousness and thought.
2. a person's intellect. Oxford Languages

COACHING PREMISES:
- ✓ Thoughts lead to actions and create our life experiences.
- ✓ We have choice over what we think and believe.
- ✓ Positive mindsets lead to more positive outcomes.
- ✓ Negative mindsets lead to more negative outcomes.

SENTIENCE:

Humans are sentient beings. We are capable of abstract thought. Our minds are creative and creating. We create outcomes and generate major portions of our future. We also can fall prey to deception in our sentience because we carry the capacity of abstract thinking. The asset can quickly turn into a liability. Our sentience gives us access to life's most amazing capacities! We are capable of art, innovation, music, humor, creation, wisdom, knowledge, intimacy, laughter, joy, love, and spirituality.

When does our sentience become a sentence? We are equally capable of building empires of illusion. Think of Hitler. A complete delusion grew an entire empire, with thousands deceived and self-deceived. The capacity for abstract thought means we can get caught in bias, linear thinking, self-deception, and we can create destruction.

Beautiful Side of Sentience	Destructive Side of Sentience
art, innovation, music, humor, creation, wisdom, knowledge, intimacy, laughter, joy, love and spirituality	Delusion, illusion, bias, reactivity, negative, destruction, linear thinking, self-deception

The side we engage is up to us.

THE EGO – THE CONSTRUCTS OF THE MIND

Oh, the ego. The primary message of the ego: "I am me. You are you. Therefore, we are separate."

While the ego's premise is true, its premise only is valid within a minor context of who we are. The ego's premise pertains only to the physical aspect. It is imperative to understand the nature and role of the ego to become masterful as a coach. Masterful coaches see beyond the shenanigans of the egoic-patterned ways of beings and into the heart of our clients.

In truth, we are within a body. We have a physical nature. Our body is indeed physically separate from other bodies in form. Yet, if we stop there, we absolutely will experience our separateness. The bigger truth is that our minds and hearts are connected.

Quantum physics discovered we are connected. What I do carries impact. If I was completely separate from you, I could not impact you. The bigger truth of our interconnectivity and relativity can be seen and experienced from psychological, spiritual, and quantum physics perspectives. We reach our potential when we live through the truth of who we are and we release our limitations, the egoic/limited version of our life, thoughts, and solutions.

When we examine imbalance, we see two ways our egoic self takes reality and twists it. Imbalance occurs with lack of, or an overage of. The ego is no exception. It operates from deficiencies (not enough) and overages (too much).

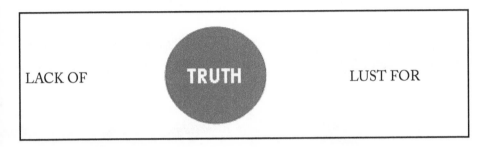

The ego gets us caught in fears or fantasies. This is fundamental to understand as a coach. Know that any illusions generated by your client can only have one of these two foundations. This is how we invite clients out of an imbalance and back to their wholeness. To live through the egoic self is to live in a constant state of fragmentation, which is experienced as a state of imbalance, big or small. When the ego equates itself with the physical form of the body, it feels limited and separate. This naturally generates fear and beliefs in limitation and separateness.

On the other side, when the egoic self sees it is winning at being separate, it can become hyper-focused on self-indulgence or self-importance. From fear, judgment is born. Through fantasy, greed is born.

The ego is incapable of operating through wholeness. Only in the heart do we experience wholeness. To the mind, wholeness is just a concept.

The ego's version of safety is positioned on the "I" in relation to the "you" while true safety is embedded in the "we." True safety comes from our responsiveness to what is and that includes our interconnectedness.

Masterful living embodies an awareness of egoic self:
- "Yes, I did want the dessert all to myself."
- "I really don't care what happens to him."
- "What was done was unforgivable."

All solutions of the ego contain an "I" bias. All solutions of the ego aren't really solutions. What part of you is viewing life? Your whole self or egoic self.

The ego cannot solve the problems of the ego. But it thinks it can. Its solutions are naturally limited or limiting. Instead of learning to live through the ego, learn to see through the ego.

Beyond the limit is the summit.

Let's look at steps that help our clients reach their summit. We are hired to help them step out of the illusions crafted by the egoic self and learn how to embrace their essence.

STEP ONE: Egoic Awareness

The first step out of the ego requires us to develop an awareness of the fears and defenses of the ego. As we step out of fear, our wholeness does appear. Wholeness never goes away. The ego is the fast track into illusion. The ego will shape its beliefs to accommodate its needs; those needs are always self-serving. The ego lives through a lens of fear and defenses. Even its lusts are ways to remain "safe." The lenses of the ego are many.

The essence has no lens; it sees all things for what they are.

Essence says:
"It is what it is."

Ego says:
"It is what it isn't."

The lens of fear acts like a filter. Fear filters out full possibilities and full understanding. Fear incidentally determines the box we place ourselves in. The truth is, we all have an egoic self. This is what it is. As long as we are in a physical body, we will have an egoic self. The question is: Are we aware of the egoic self? Once we can see it, we no longer have to be it.

We step out of the box when we realize the box does not exist. Stepping outside of the box, we are free to see and to be who we choose with our wholeness as the pilot.

STEP TWO: Embracing the Essence

There comes a time when the constriction of remaining a bud no longer feels good, and we decide it's time to blossom. What does it mean to live through our wholeness? What does it mean to act through our essence? What does it mean to extend who we truly are out into the world?

As we embrace our essence of who we really are, we realize the box constructed to protect us is the same box of our limitations. This embrace is where our empowerment and freedom are found. As we step out of an illusion, the truth gladly illuminates a new path and we live unclouded in complete understanding of "what is" so that we can then choose "what can be."

We can remain years, decades, and lifetimes bouncing around the constructs of the ego. Its mirrors and valleys and landscapes do not stop. The ego can keep us on an emotional rollercoaster. "I'm safe." "I am not." "I am successful." "I am a phony." "I am good." "I am bad." To live through any lens of the egoic self has constructed is exhaustive. The egoic self truly struggles through effort and striving and is not capable of genuinely thriving. Our essence carries all inner knowing, and through this knowing, we begin truly growing.

To "learn" through the ego is equally exhausting. All the ways the ego shows up grow and grow, year in and year out. Every circumstance the ego comes up with a new story. The ego is a shape-shifter, shifting to each situation, adapting new ways and ideals to keep you "safe" to keep you from genuine connection. Its story is that true connection is vulnerable.

The problem? Ego sight is limited. Essence is limitless.

Can full potential ever be found in limitation? Can an illusion ever be true? Can a half-truth ever be a full truth? In truth, there is only your essence, your true self. In truth, there is only truth, there is no illusion.

The ego's version of any virtue is distorted and distorting. "Success" through the egoic lens means I have more than you, more visibility, or money, or fame. "Mastery" through the egoic self means I am better than you. Yet, the essence knows we are all doing our best. When we know better, we do better. "Wealth" through the egoic lens means I have more money than you, and I want more for myself than I wish for another. Yet, the essence sees true wealth is everywhere, and real abundance is meant to be shared!

Getting to "the top" by virtue of the ego is a truly lonely endeavor. As you push aside others and live through the "I," there is no authentic connection to be found. Guess where we feel the most fulfilled? In connection. When we reach the end of our life and are ready to take our last breath, will our hearts smile from living fulfilled and connected, or will we face regret because we lived in the limit?

True mastery is the art of seeing all things as they are and as they can be.

Instead of fighting against life and trying to learn the thousands of ways the ego shows up so you can be one step ahead and master your life, learn one thing and one thing alone:

The difference between
the truth and an illusion.

Understanding truth is the one true wisdom that all other wisdom stands upon.

"Ye shall know the truth,
and the truth shall make you free."
John, 8:32

Let go of trying to manage the ego, which is exhausting and exhaustive. Instead, step out of the ego and embrace your essence. Step out of the illusion and into the truth. Step out of the limit and you will find the limitless.

STEP THREE: Expand Your Life

As you embrace your essence and potential, you will expand towards your potential instead of fractioning off from it. Expand life from your wholeness. When you experience life lived through your wholeness, you will know it because you will feel love, loved, and loving in new ways.

THE THIRD GATEWAY - THE HUMAN SPIRIT

"You think with your head. You know with your heart."
Book of Longings, by Sue Kidd-Monk

For centuries, and across cultures, humans have had a relationship with the human spirit, the heart. Our language is rich with reflections of the heart:

"Home is where the heart is."
"Absence makes the heart grow fonder." "My heart is broken."
"My heart bleeds for her."
"Let's get to the heart of the matter."

"My heart hurts over this." "Follow your heart!"
"He has a pure heart."
"My heart is filled with joy!"
"I am grateful you took this to heart."

When you miss someone, where do you feel the longing? After you go through a breakup, what part of you hurts? The concept of the heart being the true essence of a person is not new or unique. Yet, it is often overlooked or brushed off. How you define "heart" metaphorically represents the part of you that carries your answers and is most wise.

The heart of your client is their:
- Wholeness
- Essence
- Highest self
- True self
- Internal compass

In a spiritual, or religious sense, some philosophies equate the heart with having a soul that surpasses the death of the body. In atheistic philosophies, the heart is symbolic only of our capacity for spirituality.

Despite your relationship, definition, or language used, there is a part in each human being that reflects our truth, our potential, our essence, and this part carries our greatest wisdom. This is the part you want to engage with your client.

> *"The greatest treasures are invisible by the eye*
> *but found by the heart."*
> Angie Karan

> *"For where your treasure is,*
> *there your heart will be."*
> Luke 12:34

> *"You will never ever reach your*
> *full potential if you don't open your heart."*
> – Paulo Coelho

Animals have a sixth sense. Science has found that humans do, too; however, humans are so distracted with cell phones, emails, progress obsession, consumption, and taxes that many of us have never developed a keen awareness of our full capacities. Science has found that the heart is also physically connected to something much greater.

In the documentary *The Power of the Heart*, Rollin McCraty is interviewed about his research on the heart and how information flows from heart to brain. In this study, participants were hooked up to brain, skin, and heart monitors. Each person was shown thirty random high or low arousal images. An image popped up for three seconds, then was blank for ten seconds. The results were completely unexpected. The heart reacted to the images before the brain or skin even. But, what shocked the scientists most was not logically explainable by physical science: *the heart clearly reacted before the person visually saw.* What was even more unexplainable is that *the heart reacted five seconds prior to the high arousal pictures being randomly chosen by a computer program.*

That experiment demonstrated that the heart always responds first, then the brain, then the body last. This study also suggests the heart is connected to a form of intuition not bound by time/space. Surface science, which requires measurement, would tell us this is impossible; however, normal laws of space and time do not apply when science gets into the quantum realm. Energy is subject to its own laws, many of which have not yet been discovered and are not yet understood! Powerful.

Maya Angelo spoke of wanting a million dollars and how the mind [ego] may lead you to rob a bank. The heart says, "Put down your fears and follow me. I'll show you the way." The heart's solutions do not cause harm. The heart crafts win-wins and will never say, "I want more for myself than I do for my brother."

If the heart is connected to something greater, are we brave enough to trust it?

℘ CONCLUSION ℘

As we wrap up our time together, we will explore the ways to continue along the path of mastery. If you are inviting your clients to integrate, how can you invite yourself to integrate?

There are many paths to the top of the same mountain. In conclusion, I invite you to consider your relationship to receiving mentoring and supervision. These are two powerful ways to enhance your capacity as a coach. Those are also pathways to develop MCC levels of masterful presence and responsiveness.

Let's wrap up by exploring integration, voice, and vision.

INTEGRATING AS A COACH

I have good news and bad news.

Let's start with the good news: *Mastery is not about perfection.*

OK, now the bad news: *Mastery is not about perfection.*

Yes, it is both.

On one hand what a relief that mastery is not about being perfect. Perfect is a pipe dream. On the other hand, what a bummer. You mean there isn't a plateau I reach and then "poof" I'm done? Mastery is *not* perfection. Mastery is our capacity to respond through our capacity. Do not try to be perfect or get everything 100% "right." Instead, hold the space of presence to respond to what is needed. What is needed is ever-changing; our ability to respond is to live masterfully.

I invite you to go back over each section as you grow as a coach. As you do, it will take you to a new level of understanding and absorb even deeper. To integrate as a coach, I invite you to take all of the practices formulated to help you gain mastery and apply them to yourself first.

All good coaches also have coaches. Potential is ironic because the minute we define it, we also limit it. Being in coaching helps us continue to unfold new layers of ourselves and our potentials.

There are also levels of support for coaches that go beyond training and having your own coach. There are also mentor coaches and coaching supervision programs.

Let's explore these next so you can discover the best path of skill integration for you.

GROWING WITH MENTORING & SUPERVISION

Mentoring and supervision are both processes and services that support coaching mastery. Both mentoring and supervision are provided in high-quality ICF-accredited coach training programs. They each serve a different purpose and help coaches grow their coaching success to the next level.

We can't fix what we don't see. When we are self-referenced, it is harder to grow. This is because:

There are things we know.
There are things we do not know.
There are things we know that we know.

There are things that we know that we don't know.
(I know that I do not know how to fly an airplane.)
Then, there are the things that we do not know that we do not know.

This is where supervisors and mentors come in to help us grow.

Why not take a shortcut and stand upon the shoulders of those that have come before you and are here to impart their hard-earned wisdom to help you elevate sooner? This is also why it is ineffective to learn coaching from a textbook. Would you go to a surgeon that was self-taught through books?

Below is an overview that outlines the distinctions to each approach.

MENTOR COACHING

Mentors help you develop in-session success.

The ICF identifies two methods of mentoring: private mentoring and group mentoring. In Group Mentor Coaching, an ICF-trained mentor reviews a live practice session with a group of observers. Mentors are objective observers that can help you identify areas of mastery and offer encouragement in any areas of growth.

In group sessions, mentors look for:
- Competencies
- Opportunities

Purpose: Group mentoring is a safe and supportive space to practice the phase of coaching skills being worked on. In groups, everyone benefits from seeing a variety of coaching approaches and discussing the skills observed.

Private Mentor Coaching is a process where an ICF-trained mentor reviews a recorded session and gives you in-depth, detailed feedback on your coaching skills.

Mentors are trained as objective observers who can help you identify areas of mastery and offer direction in any areas of skill growth.

Mentors:
- Coaching Competencies
- Natural abilities
- Patterns
- Opportunities

Areas of Competency: These are observable coaching skills that are already showing up in a session in response to the client's offers. It is best to keep in mind not all skills will apply to every session. A mentor coach is looking for a well-rounded approach in a session.

Natural Ability: A mentor coach may observe skills the coach is doing well, and quite naturally, and reflect those back. Natural ability can be helpful to the coaching unless it is a pattern that might keep you single-focused. The mentor feedback helps the coach see when a natural ability is an asset and when it may be an ability.

Patterns: Mentors are trained to pick up on any patterns the coach may or may not be aware of. Patterns can inhibit a coach's ability to use a full scope of skills and approaches. Mentoring is an opportunity to locate and shift any patterns that may hinder your mastery.

Opportunities: As we progress in coaching mastery, there are always opportunities to grow our skills, abilities, and approaches. In mentoring, various techniques and frameworks are identified so that the coach may explore a fuller spectrum of their potential. Mentors go into the nuances of wording, framing, and approach.

Purpose: Since we can't fix what we don't see, mentors help us see our potential by offering objective observation, reflection, and exploration. Mentoring helps us expand our capacity and scope as a masterful coach.

Learning the small distinctions helps coaches create finely tuned coaching habits early on and prevents "bad" habits from forming over time.

Some examples:

Helpful Habits	Hampering Habits
• One question at a time • Interrupting with a purpose • Quiet listening	• Multiple questions • Interrupting to share your idea • Adding to silence "Ok" "Uh-huh"

COACHING SUPERVISION

Supervision is much broader in scope than mentoring. Supervision covers coaching success beyond the session.

Mentoring is specific to in-session coaching skills and competencies. Supervision covers anything outside of a session that helps you succeed and develop as a professional coach.

Supervision includes ethical questions, policies, processes, business practices, cultural sensitives, and exploring the lines of personal bias. A supervisor is hired to support your overall professional development and success.

Both supervisors and mentors can help you find and embody your coaching voice.

FINDING YOUR COACHING VOICE
Finding your coaching voice and presence develops over time.

Your coaching voice brings to life your coaching gifts, passion for empowering and your unique style. Your voice is how you share your calling with the world.

"No two sets of values, principles, vision, and skills – are alike.
Whether you are a CEO,

team leader, [coach] or entrepreneur, you need to discover who you are as a leader,
what you believe, and how that defines you. "
— Suzanne Bates

As a coach you are the leader. A servant leader. You lead by following. Knowing who you are and what you stand for as a coach helps attract your clients to you. Being clear enables you to steer.

Developing your presence as a professional coach will help you:
* Attract your ideal clients
* Elevate your impact
* Retain clients year after year
* Create business opportunities
* Leave a positive legacy
* Be known as a "go to"

Beyond what we cover in coach training class, I invite you to discover the processes that Suzanne Bates covers in her book *Discover Your CEO Brand: Secrets to Embracing & Maximizing your Unique Value as a Leader.*

The exercises in her branding book about being a leader also translate to coaches. Her processes can help you craft your own unique coaching message, understand the power of your presence, and shape your unique "brand" or style of coaching.

You are invited to step into a new vision when developing your voice, brand, and presence.

CULTIVATING A NEW VISION

There are two stories we can live through. Stories of victimhood or stories of warriorhood. The stories we take with us have shaped us throughout our life. The stories we live through encompass our very unique life experiences.

Masterful coaches invite our clients to step beyond stories and into vision.

Our stories are full of how we have interpreted our strife's and our victories. Our stories contain elements of how we were a victim and how we became a victor. While the past is the past, there is a new story waiting. It does not tell a tale. It is a story that uses the past to pave a new path. I invite you to now step out of the story and into your glory. I invite you to take your mission and craft a new vision.

I invite you to step into *vision*.
Vision is the birthplace of your *mastery*.
Vision puts you at *the inception point* of possibility.

As you choose the direction, you pave the path to a new outcome. The bridge taken from "story" to "vision" answers a single question:

What do you wish to come of this?

Temet Nosce

Know Thyself

❦ REFERENCES ❧

1. Altman, J. (2017, January 19). *How Much Does Employee Turnover Really Cost?* HuffPost. https://www.huffpost.com/entry/how-much-does-employee-turnover-really- cost_b_587fbaf9e4b0474ad4874fb7
2. *Aristotle's Biology.* (2021, July 16). Stanford Encyclopedia of Philosophy. https://plato.stanford.edu/entries/aristotle-biology/
3. C. (2018, February 21). *Who invented the first car?* Curious History. https://www.curioushistory.com/who-invented-the-first-car/
4. Coelho, P. (2021). *The Alchemist by Coelho, Paulo (Author)Apr-25-2006 Paperback.* HarperTorch.
5. Covey, S. R. (2006). *The 8th Habit: From Effectiveness to Greatness by Covey. Stephen R. (2006) Paperback* (New edition). Simon & Schuster.
6. *The Components of MI.* (n.d.). MI Oasis. Retrieved August 8, 2021, from https://www.multipleintelligencesoasis.org/the-components-of-mi
7. Belf, Marx. (2017, December 8). *From the Toolbox: Do you give advice to your Clients?* International Coaching Federation. https://coachingfederation.org/blog/from-the-toolbox-do-you-give-advice-to- your-clients
8. Gunnarson, J. (2020, October 19). *Eckhart on the Dark Night of the Soul | by Eckhart Tolle.* Eckhart Tolle | Official Site - Spiritual Teachings and Tools For Personal Growth and Happiness. https://eckharttolle.com/eckhart-on-the-dark-night-of-the-soul/
9. Harvard Health. (2020, July 6). *Understanding the stress response.* https://www.health.harvard.edu/staying-healthy/understanding-the-stress-response

10. Jabr, F. (2012, August 10). *How Does a Caterpillar Turn into a Butterfly?* Scientific American. https://www.scientificamerican.com/article/caterpillar-butterfly-metamorphosis-explainer/

11. Jones, L. B. (1998). *Jesus In Blue Jeans: A Practical Guide To Everyday Spirituality* (First Edition). Hyperion.

12. Mindbodygreen. (2021, March 2). *How To Use Your Intuition Like A Professional Psychic.* https://www.mindbodygreen.com/articles/the-4-types-of-intuition-and-how-to-tap-into-each

13. Mosher, C. (2014, December 23). *How to Grow Stronger Without Lifting Weights.* Scientific American. https://www.scientificamerican.com/article/how-to-grow-stronger-without-lifting-weights/

14. Riggio, R. (2012, June 25). *There's Magic in Your Smile.* Psychology Today. https://www.psychologytoday.com/us/blog/cutting-edge-leadership/201206/there-s-magic-in-your- smile

15. Smith, H. W. (1995). *10 Natural Laws of Successful Time and Life Management.* Business Plus.

16. Waters, Chiu, Atkinson, Dirk Blom, F. V. A. J. (2018, July 10). *Severe Sleep Deprivation Causes Hallucinations and a Gradual Progression Toward Psychosis With Increasing Time Awake.* Frontiers in Psychiatry. https://www.ncbi.nlm.nih.gov/pmc/articles/PMC6048360

17. Wikipedia contributors. (2021a, May 30). *Howard Gardner.* Wikipedia. https://en.wikipedia.org/wiki/Howard_Gardner

18. Wikipedia contributors. (2021, July 23). *Yin and yang.* Wikipedia. https://en.wikipedia.org/wiki/Yin_and_yang

19. Wikipedia contributors. (2021c, July 26). *Allopathic medicine.* Wikipedia. https://en.wikipedia.org/wiki/Allopathic_medicine

20. Wikipedia contributors. (2021b, August 7). *René Descartes.* Wikipedia. https://en.wikipedia.org/wiki/Ren%C3%A9_Descartes